WALTER WANGER *and* JOE HYAMS

MY LIFE WITH CLEOPATRA

Walter Wanger, the producer of *Cleopatra*, attended Dartmouth, served as a reconnaissance pilot with the Signal Corps of the U.S. Army in Italy in WWI, was appointed attaché to the American Peace Mission headed by President Wilson, and attended the Paris Peace Conference. In the early 1920s, Wanger worked at Paramount Studios where he acquired the novel *The Sheik*, which was made into a successful film starring Rudolph Valentino. After a brief hiatus in England, Wanger returned to Paramount where he was general manager of production from 1924 to 1931. He was president of the Academy of Motion Picture Arts and Sciences from 1939 to 1941, for which he received an Honorary Academy Award in 1946. The producer of more than sixty motion pictures, including the first outdoor color film and *Queen Christina*, *Scarlet Street*, *Stagecoach*, *Foreign Correspondent*, *I Want to Live*, and *The Invasion of the Body Snatchers*, he worked with such directors as John Ford, Alfred Hitchcock, George Cukor, Victor Fleming, Fritz Lang, and Don Siegel; and such stars as Ingrid Bergman, the Marx Brothers, Henry Fonda, Charles Boyer, Cary Grant, Claudette Colbert, Fredric March, Susan Hayward, and Greta Garbo. He married Justine Johnson, a Ziegfield Girl, and later the actress Joan Bennett with whom he had two daughters. He died in 1968.

Joe Hyams was a Hollywood columnist, former movie editor of *This Week* magazine, and Hollywood correspondent for the *New York Herald Tribune*. He was the author or co-author of over two dozen books, many of which are bestselling biographies of Hollywood stars. He died in 2008.

MY LIFE WITH CLEOPATRA

MY LIFE WITH CLEOPATRA

The Making of a Hollywood Classic

WALTER WANGER

and

JOE HYAMS

Afterword by

KENNETH TURAN

Vintage Books
A Division of Random House, Inc. | *New York*

FIRST VINTAGE BOOKS EDITION, JUNE 2013

The Cataloging-in-Publication data is on file at the Library of Congress.

Vintage ISBN: 978-0-345-80405-1

www.vintagebooks.com

146028962

To my daughters
Stephanie and Shelley
who wanted to know
what a producer does

CONTENTS

PROLOGUE

What I have to say in this book may shock some hypocrites and offend some moralists. This is not to imply that my book is a deliberate attempt to provoke controversy. The controversy was already there.

I have been told by responsible journalists that there was more world interest in *Cleopatra*, which I produced, and in its stars—Elizabeth Taylor, Richard Burton, and Rex Harrison—than in any other news event of 1962.

Cleopatra is not only the most written about motion picture in history, but it was also the most talked about. As you will discover, never have so many people known so little about a subject which, obviously, intrigued them.

What emerges in these pages is my story of the most expensive and perhaps greatest motion picture in film history. As the producer, I had a bird's-eye view of the whole operation, plus a certain degree of detachment. I must add here, however, that I saw the happenings of the four hectic years the film was in production only through the eyes of the producer. I am neither a journalist nor a moralist. My concern was always that of a man who measured everything against one yardstick—how will this affect the picture and Elizabeth Taylor, who *is* the picture?

Making a motion picture about Cleopatra had always been a dream of mine. I first became aware of the Egyptian queen, so beautiful and wise that she almost ruled the world, when, as an undergraduate at Dartmouth almost half a century ago, I read

Théophile Gautier's story, "One of Cleopatra's Nights." That started me reading everything I could find about her—from Plutarch's *Life of Antony* in North's excellent translation to Shakespeare's classic, one of the great tales of human love.

My interest continued long after I became a motion-picture producer in Hollywood. During the next forty years and sixty pictures I cherished a hope that I could one day make a film about Cleopatra.

But there was one major problem. Who could play Cleopatra? I visualized her as more than just a great actress. She had to be the quintessence of youthful femininity, of womanliness and strength.

I saw Eleonora Duse, Sarah Bernhardt, and Ellen Terry, but by the time they had reached stardom they were too old to play Cleopatra. Then, some years ago, I saw Elizabeth Taylor in *A Place in the Sun*. I was overwhelmed. Despite the modern clothes and dialogue, she came through to me as the one young actress who could play Cleopatra. She is the only woman I have ever known who has the necessary youth, power, and emotion.

Here was my Cleopatra. From then on I never lost sight of my goal. A while later, I bought *The Life and Times of Cleopatra*, a book by Carlo Maria Franzero, for $15,000—a modest beginning for the most expensive picture of all time.

Eventually I moved to 20th Century-Fox. My first project to go into work was *Cleopatra*. As you will soon see, the studio executives were opposed to the kind of large-scale motion picture I wanted to make and to Elizabeth Taylor as its high-salaried star.

The lack of enthusiasm did not deter me. As I see it, the most important function of an independent producer such as myself is to find material that he believes will interest the public all over the world. Like any creative artist, he must be prepared for and even expect opposition when he wants to do something different and important. As my own experience proves, a producer must be ready to battle for what he believes in.

I remember that when I first proposed *The Sheik* to Paramount they were shocked, as a love story between a white woman and an Arab was considered too radical. The movie not only made a star of Rudolph Valentino, but it made millions.

There was studio opposition when I bought *An American Tragedy* from Theodore Dreiser for $90,000 at a time when every film had to have a happy ending, and the word "tragedy" in a title was anathema.

The Paramount sales department was in an uproar when I purchased *Beau Geste*, which had no love story and was, to boot, a French title.

The Technicolor Corporation warned me they would not be responsible for the result if I took a Technicolor camera out of the studio to film *The Trail of the Lonesome Pine*, because they couldn't control the light. This first outdoor color spectacular was so successful it opened up a multi-million-dollar market for Technicolor, who were so grateful they gave me stock bonuses.

Another case in point is *I Want to Live!* my last picture before *Cleopatra*. I made it in opposition to pressures from police, politicians, and press, as well as the studios. Nevertheless, Susan Hayward received an Academy Award for her brilliant portrayal of Barbara Graham.

During the making of *Cleopatra*, however, I received more than my anticipated share of opposition. Certainly, no novel I have ever read about Hollywood had as many fantastic crises, hair-breadth escapes, personal melodramas, and as much executive-suitesmanship as can be found here.

I began writing this book some time ago with Joe Hyams. Day after day for many weeks we studied the reams of newsprint and millions of words written about *Cleopatra*. Together, we interviewed many of the people who worked in the film. Then, Joe's probing questions, based on his own research and interviews in Hollywood, helped me reconstruct all the pertinent events of my life with *Cleopatra*.

Although the book is in journal form and we have attempted to be accurate with all the dates, some events could not be pinpointed. The majority of the dates are, however, as accurate as my memory allows.

Why did *Cleopatra* cost so much and take so long to film?

These were our basic problems.

We were forced to try to produce the film without being properly prepared—before we had a script or a well-thought-out and practical production plan or organization. These factors alone cost us millions of dollars in wasted time, in scrapped sets, in false starts and costly commitments.

There was a continuing problem brought on by the fact that the studio had lost more than $60,000,000 in the past few years. Consequently, the jockeying for power among the incumbent Board of Directors and minority stockholders resulted in conflicting, expensive, on-again, off-again decisions from on-again, off-again groups in power.

In addition to being the star of the picture, Elizabeth was also a partner in the enterprise. People who read fan magazines may be surprised to learn of the Elizabeth Taylor who is a real professional concerned with every aspect of picture making. She will receive over two million dollars for her role, but she is worth every penny of it.

I don't believe the general public is aware of what a star brings to a movie in addition to a great box-office following. When you deal with a star like Elizabeth or the late Marilyn Monroe or Marlon Brando or William Holden, you get what you pay for: an extraordinary talent who brings something to a movie in terms of experience and intelligence that you cannot get otherwise—if you treat them properly.

When Elizabeth Taylor walks onto a movie set, you know she is a great artist; not just in the acting sense, but in her sense of values. She not only knows her lines letter-perfect, but she has a built-in radar that divines problems in art direction or costumes or a headdress or a set.

She is honest. You always know where you stand with her. There are no games to play, no hedging, no subterfuge. She speaks directly and in a vocabulary that allows no confusion as to meaning.

People have asked me why studios tolerate the special problems that arise through dealing with such special people. The answer to that was best expressed by director Billy Wilder. After finishing a Marilyn Monroe picture that was plagued by Marilyn's illnesses and lateness, he said, "I have a healthy aunt in Vienna who would come on set on time, know her lines, and always be ready. But no one would pay to see her at the box office."

A motion picture can be conceived by a genius; the lines may be written by a spellbinder and delivered by great actors. But what is usually forgotten is the contribution made by the film technicians who are responsible for getting the image and sound and background on the screen. *Cleopatra* is a monument to the imagination and devotion of hundreds of technicians from Hollywood, London, and Rome who, despite continual crises, regularly accomplished the impossible.

In this account I have been severe on the studio executives who made my job as producer of the picture an obstacle race. I am bitter indeed about what I consider to be their bungling interference.

In retrospect, however, I can say that I understand that they were operating, for the most part, out of insecurity and fear. They were desperate, nervous men, trying to protect the studio from further losses, and *Cleopatra* soon became their scapegoat.

Despite our woes, the anger, the backbiting, the small personal tragedies and the enormous pressure from the studio as well as the press, the making of *Cleopatra* was an incredible adventure.

I feel that the film which 20th Century-Fox once complained was going to destroy the studio is probably what will save the studio. I am convinced *Cleopatra* will be a success—a great motion picture to be seen not just this year, but a classic to be seen by succeeding generations.

BOOK I

BEGINNINGS

[1958–1959]

— NEW YORK —

SEPTEMBER 30, 1958

Had my first meeting about *Cleopatra* with Spyros Skouras, president of 20th Century-Fox.

"*Cleopatra* was one of the best pictures we ever made," he said in his thick Greek accent, an expansive smile radiating good will and confidence. "Just give me this over again and we'll make a lot of money."

I was surprised. The picture he was referring to was the old silent film with Theda Bara. My face must have disclosed my feelings, because a circlet of amber beads—Greek worry beads—suddenly appeared in his left hand. They began to click-click like knitting needles. The warmth left the smile, though the mouth held the pose.

His right hand, which always hovers near the switches on the intercom adjoining his desk, punched a switch. The box enables him to make direct contact with anyone in the 20th Century-Fox operation on either coast. It is the lifeline of the operation of which he is president. Not only did he have direct contact to both coasts, but he had a passion for telephoning all over the world; picking up the phone and talking to Cairo or London or Zurich.

I heard a buzz in the reception room. "Bring me the *Cleopatra* script," he whispered. Skouras generally whispers in his office, where he is supreme commander. He sometimes bellows on the telephone. It is as though he is not as sure of the mechanical device as he is of the power of his own voice, developed when he was a child herding sheep in the Greek hills.

A secretary brought the script in, handling it gingerly—and with good reason. It was almost old enough to be made of parchment.

"All this needs is a little rewriting," Spyros said, waving me out of the office.

I examined the script while leaving Fox's old West Side quarters, which look so much like a car barn. It was only a few pages long and, since it was a silent film, the dialogue was for subtitles. Most of the writing was concerned with camera setups.

Joseph Moskowitz, executive vice-president of the studio, a dapper, cold, right-hand man to Skouras, drove uptown with me. "Who needs a Liz Taylor," he said. "Any hundred-dollar-a-week girl can play Cleopatra."

— HOLLYWOOD —

OCTOBER 20, 1958

My first day at the studio. Lunched with Lew Schreiber, general production manager.

It has been almost twenty years since I had worked as a producer at a major studio which still operated like Fox. At one time or another I had been with nearly all of them—MGM, RKO, Paramount, Eagle-Lion, Universal, and United Artists. However, I functioned as an independent producer in charge of my own company with autonomy.

At lunch in the studio's executive dining room, Lew Schreiber reminded me of the rules for operating within an old-fashioned studio operation.

Don't talk directly to agents about anyone or anything.

Talk only with Schreiber or Buddy Adler, the studio head; if they approve my ideas, they will take them up with New York where final decisions are made.

Don't talk with writers without first going to David Brown, studio story editor, for his opinion.

Don't talk to actors without going to the casting department first.

In short, a very different operation from my last independent production, *I Want to Live*! It was my idea, and I hired the writers to develop the story, engaged the star and director and most of the staff, was responsible for the budget, and acted as consultant on merchandising, advertising, and publicity.

I was not an employee of Fox—technically, I was on loan from my own production company—but I was soon made painfully aware that even the so-called independent producer at a major studio must be prepared to accept committee rule and interference. I wasn't looking forward to the struggle ahead but knew it was inevitable.

October 22, 1958

Buddy Adler told me at lunch today we can make *Cleopatra* for about a million or a million-two, with Joan Collins.

I protested that if the picture was going to be done properly—I visualized it as a picture with great scope—it would have to have locations and would cost at least two million dollars.

"All right, if you don't want to make it, I'll get somebody else to produce it for eight hundred thousand," he said testily. "This type of picture isn't my cup of tea anyhow."

With a heart like mine, getting angry is one luxury I can't afford. What I wanted to produce was a "blockbuster." To Buddy, *Cleopatra* sounded like just another sex-and-sand epic.

The only thing that appealed to him was the possibility it offered of using some of the contract stars—Joan Collins, Joanne Woodward, or Suzy Parker. And, if it was made on the lot, it would keep some of the other contract people busy: cameramen, grips, electricians. The problem Buddy had was a big studio with a lot of people under contract and many stages which he had to keep full. He had to feed his distribution organization with film. That was the old plan the major studios functioned under, and that was what Skouras kept pressing him to do. That's why the quicker the picture was started and finished and the cheaper it was produced, the better it was for all concerned—except the creators and the audience.

I was more than willing to discount Buddy's testiness. He was a good friend and a good picture maker, but I had heard rumors that he was a very sick man. In fact, when my contract was negotiated, it was taken to him in the hospital for approval.

NOVEMBER 1958

Made an appointment with Liz Taylor, to see if I could revive her interest in *Cleopatra*.

I had first approached Liz when she was married to Mike Todd. To me, she is one of the most amazing women of our time—really a modern Cleopatra. She was enthusiastic, said Cleopatra had always fascinated her. But she was letting Mike make decisions because she didn't want to take an assignment that would separate them, and I planned to make the movie on location.

I went to see Mike at the old Chaplin Studios where he was finishing *Around the World in Eighty Days*. He took me into the projection room to see the first cut of the picture. I never got an answer from him about *Cleopatra*, but I gave him the book *The Life and Times of Cleopatra* to give to Elizabeth to read.

Soon after my meeting with Todd he died in the tragic plane crash. The only time I had seen Elizabeth since was once when I was flying to La Jolla taking my daughter to school and she got on the plane with her brother. I almost didn't recognize her. She was in mourning and looked miserable. We spoke for only a moment.

When I telephoned Liz today, she said she would be at the Polo

Lounge of the Beverly Hills Hotel, having a drink with Arthur Loew, Jr. I dropped by for a brief moment, chatted with her and Arthur, who is the son of an old friend of mine, and left the book for Elizabeth to read. Evidently Mike had never given it to her.

Then I returned to my office and called her agent, Kurt Frings, and her lawyer, Martin Gang, to tell them I wanted her for the picture and had given her the book.

NOVEMBER 1958

Told Lew Schreiber I had given the book to Elizabeth Taylor. He was upset.

I think Schreiber feels that my independence is somehow a threat to the studio—maybe he thinks it might influence other producers to get out of line. He said I had no right to go over his head and approach a star directly. The studio wouldn't have Elizabeth Taylor in a picture.

DECEMBER 1958

First steps.

David Brown approved my request to start someone writing a script of *Cleopatra*. Ludi Claire, an actress turned writer, is going to assemble material and do a rough script, the least expensive way to start a project.

I have asked John DeCuir, an excellent art director, to do some sketches and models of the Forum and the palace, in the hope that the studio executives will see some of the possibilities in size and scope of the picture.

FEBRUARY 1959

Although Skouras thinks Joanne Woodward is the biggest female attraction in the movies, thanks to *Three Faces of Eve*, Adler is insistent we use Joan Collins, who is physically right for the role and is dying to play it. Dance director Hermes Pan is working with Joan, trying to improve her posture and walk so she will have the grace and dignity of Cleopatra.

FEBRUARY 14, 1959

John DeCuir's sketches and models were finished, and I had a display set up on one of the test stages behind the art department. All the executives were invited over after lunch to look them over.

The plaster model of the Forum took up almost an entire table top, the sketches and models were beautiful. I'm continually amazed at the great skills of the artisans on the Hollywood back lots.

For the first time, I think Adler and Schreiber see what I really have in mind for *Cleopatra*.

It can be the last word in opulence, beauty, and art—a picture women will love for its beauty and story. After all, it is the story of a woman who almost ruled the world but was destroyed by love. With the right cast and production values, the right director and script, this can be a sensation. The material is fantastic. The more of it I read, the better I like it.

FEBRUARY 16, 1959

Still testing.

The casting department has compiled a list of possibilities for each role. Submitting these names is their job. The function of a producer is to argue out and prove to the casting department why some individuals don't fit the picture and why certain combinations aren't good. My first team is Liz Taylor as Cleopatra, Sir Laurence Olivier as Caesar, and Richard Burton as Mark Antony. The ideal box-office team, according to them, would be Cary Grant as Caesar, Elizabeth Taylor as Cleopatra, and Burt Lancaster as Mark Antony.

Other actors submitted by casting for Caesar are Sir John Gielgud, Yul Brynner, and Curt Jurgens.

For Cleopatra, they have listed Brigitte Bardot, Marilyn Monroe, Jennifer Jones, Kim Novak, Audrey Hepburn, Sophia Loren, Gina Lollobrigida, and Susan Hayward. Some contract actresses being recommended seriously are Joan Collins, Dolores Michaels, Millie Perkins, Barbara Steele, and Suzy Parker.

The group being suggested for Antony includes Anthony Franciosa, Kirk Douglas, Marlon Brando, Stephen Boyd, Jason Robards, Jr., Richard Basehart, and Richard Burton.

February 24, 1959

On my own I had lunch with Carlo Ponti, Sophia Loren's husband, at Perino's Restaurant.

Since my Italian is not too good and his English is poor, I took Rosemary Mathews along as interpreter. She was assistant to Johnny Johnston, production manager on *I Want to Live*! when I was making it.

Carlo said he was certain Sophia would be interested in doing the picture. Then he asked me when and where we planned to do it. When I said in July on the Studio's back lot, he answered, "You'll never make it this summer and you'll never make it in America. Italy is the only place to make it."

March 4, 1959

Nigel Balchin signed to prepare a screenplay of *Cleopatra*, with Ludi Claire's outline for a springboard.

May 12, 1959

Elizabeth married Eddie Fisher today in Las Vegas.

Elizabeth and Eddie are expected to go through New York on their way to the Mediterranean for a cruise honeymoon. Then she's going to do *Suddenly Last Summer* for Columbia and Sam Spiegel, which makes it unlikely that I'll get her for *Cleopatra*, which is supposed to start in July.

June 15, 1959

Skouras took Gina Lollobrigida and her husband to director Rouben Mamoulian's house for dinner to discuss *Cleopatra* with them both.

June 19, 1959

Received this morning a preliminary production cost estimate for *Cleopatra*, based on the script by Nigel Balchin.

The operating budget for *Cleopatra*, labeled "Production No. J—01" called for 64 days' shooting. It showed that the total cost was supposed to come to $2,955,700, without the cast or director.

July 29, 1959

The studio executives were so enthusiastic about the first-draft script by Nigel Balchin that Adler has called Kurt Frings, Elizabeth's agent, to get him to take the script abroad to Elizabeth and to Audrey Hepburn, another of his clients. Adler ended the conversation with Kurt, admonishing him not to tell me about it.

I don't know what's on Buddy's mind, trying to keep this information from me. Obviously, as Frings is a great friend of mine, he would tell me, as he knew I always wanted Elizabeth for the part.

Meanwhile, I discovered that they are excavating on the back lot with bulldozers, preparing to build the city of Alexandria. No one has asked me about this because we have never finally determined where the picture is to be filmed.

August 1959

Both Elizabeth and Audrey Hepburn have agreed to do *Cleopatra*.

Kurt Frings gave me the good news on the phone today. He just came back from visiting both of his clients in Europe.

August 18, 1959

Called Schreiber to see if there was anything definite on casting. He said, "No."

I told him that Audrey Hepburn had read the script and was interested. He seemed surprised that I knew. An hour or so later he called me back to say we can't have Hepburn because Paramount has her under contract and won't release her.

I called Skouras, who told me Elizabeth doesn't want to play Cleopatra—despite Kurt assuring me that she does.

August 27, 1959

The planned Suzy Parker test for *Cleopatra* didn't come off as scheduled. When the studio called her in New York requesting a test, she became hysterical and burst into tears. It turned out she was pregnant, a secret no one knew until today.

September 1, 1959

Called Elizabeth in London where she is doing *Suddenly Last Summer*.

She said she will do *Cleopatra* for a million dollars and a few changes in the script, and as long as the picture is not to be made in Hollywood.

Elizabeth sees Cleopatra as I do—the greatest woman's role ever written, and she thinks as I do, that this can be a great picture. When I said that a million dollars was an unheard-of price for an actress, she said that I knew as well as she did that this was going to be a long, hard picture. But she doesn't mind taking the money on a spread payment, so much per year, since she really wants it to put in trust for her children.

I called Skouras to tell him the news. He said he doesn't like the idea of working with Elizabeth because "she'll be too much trouble."

SEPTEMBER 28, 1959*

A meeting was held at the studio yesterday (Sunday), to which I was not invited—and for obvious reasons.

Spyros Skouras was there, as was Buddy Adler, Lew Schreiber, David Brown, Sid Rogell, who is in charge of studio operations, and Robert Goldstein.

It was decided, evidently, that my status on the project was to be subordinated to that of Goldstein, who would be completely in charge of the production. While I could go abroad on the production, Goldstein would be responsible for all decisions and, in the event of dispute, Buddy Adler would be the arbitrator.

It was estimated that the picture will cost between $4,500,000 and $5,000,000, with overhead including $1,300,000 for the stars and $100,000 for the director. The plan is to make the picture in London.

Rouben Mamoulian was proposed as director by Skouras, who is Rouben's old friend and has now decided he wants someone with an artistic reputation. Up to now, all they wanted was someone who was efficient and fast.

OCTOBER 8, 1959

Skouras has taken a poll of everyone at the New York office, and they all want Susan Hayward to play Cleopatra. He told me he is going to announce Susan for the role immediately.

Skouras seems determined to have a contract actress—and Susan is under contract—play Cleopatra because he hasn't much faith in the potential gross of the picture. "It can't gross really big unless it is produced at a limited cost," he told me. "Only biblical pictures can do big business today."

* Although this meeting is in its proper sequence, I did not come upon the memorandum reporting it until some months later in London.

October 9, 1959

I called Elizabeth at the Beverly Hills Hotel, to tell her she doesn't have the part and thank her for being so nice. She started to cry.

"I want to do it," she said. "Why don't they want me?"

"They won't pay a million dollars," I said.

"I'll do it for a guarantee of seven hundred and fifty thousand, against ten per cent of the gross," she said.

I called Adler, who said, "See if you can get her for six hundred thousand."

I called Lew Schreiber, Kurt Frings, Liz, and Frings again, and at last got the negotiations back on the track.

October 10, 1959

Kurt Frings is negotiating with MGM to get them to allow her to do *Cleopatra* as an outside picture. According to her contract, she has one more film to make for MGM, and they're insisting she do *Butterfield 8.*

Ironically, Elizabeth was willing to do *Cleopatra* for $750,000, but I am told Frings has now got her back to the million-dollar figure.

Elizabeth doesn't want to do *Butterfield 8.*

"The leading lady is almost a prostitute," she told me. "When I told this to Sol, he said he'd clean up the script. But she's still a sick nymphomaniac. The whole thing is so unpalatable, I wouldn't do it for anything, under any condition."

October 12, 1959

Elizabeth is in *Cleopatra* again, and *Butterfield 8* is being rewritten for her.

Frings and the Fox lawyers are busy working out details of her contract for *Cleopatra*, which will follow *Butterfield 8.* We are going to stage a contract-signing scene in Buddy Adler's office within a few days, however, to make it look official, although the real contract won't be ready for months.

Elizabeth has read the script. Her feeling is that the opening scene is forced, and that a girl—nineteen years old, with a lot of background and intelligence—should still be seeking wisdom and having qualms about her decisions. Caesar helps her make a gradual transition from a child to a woman.

She thinks the characterization needs that sense of development from beginning to end. She feels very strongly that the scenes with Caesar are a little flat and should be more lifelike, with a certain amount of charm and warmth and feeling that is lacking at the present time.

Also, she would like any research material and books I think she ought to read on the subject.

She told me she would like to have both penthouses at the Dorchester in London. She had them last time she was there and she'd like them during this picture.

We discussed cameramen, and she said she is mad about Jack Hillyard, who is now with Fred Zinnemann in Australia. I'm to check on his availability. She thinks Bluey Hill would be a great assistant director.

Elizabeth specified that she wants Sidney Guilaroff for hairdos and, as her own hairdresser, she wants a girl called Joan White. I'm to check on their availability.

I consider it most important that we try to satisfy Elizabeth on all such matters, because she is the pivot of our whole operation.

OCTOBER 15, 1959

Elizabeth "signed" for *Cleopatra* today. We took photos in Adler's office. I was delighted.

OCTOBER 1959

Schreiber called me into his office to tell me I'm not going to London when the picture is being made, but he does want me to be responsible for controlling the cost.

When I pointed out it would be impossible to produce a picture being made thousands of miles away, he said, "Jerry Wald didn't go over on *Sons and Lovers*, and the picture came out fine. There's no need for you to be in London. I want you to be preparing your next picture."

Schreiber did ask me for suggestions on a director. I think Alfred Hitchcock would be great because he would bring the right touch of suspense to the story and give it needed drama. I am a great Hitchcock fan, and I liked the picture he made for me, *Foreign Correspondent*.

OCTOBER 19, 1959

Hitch doesn't think it's his cup of tea. Saw Adler about Mamoulian, who is choice of Skouras and Schreiber.

Rouben is an old and good friend of mine—I took him from the Theater Guild in the Twenties, and he directed *Applause* for me at Paramount. Then we worked together with Garbo on *Queen Christina*.

OCTOBER 21, 1959

Rouben signed by the studio.

The moment I get in a dispute with him over something, he's going to turn around and say, "You didn't hire me. Skouras, Adler, and Schreiber did."

NOVEMBER 1959

No sooner has Rouben been hired than he has a few ideas for "little changes."

NOVEMBER 1959

Interviewed writers most of the day.

I am most interested in a new writer named James Costigan, who is in demand because of a TV show he wrote called *Little Moon of Alban*. Neither he nor Christopher Fry, whom I also contacted, is available.

NOVEMBER 25, 1959

Dale Wasserman hired, for Mamoulian feels he can work with him and liked his TV spectacular *Don Quixote*.

NOVEMBER 1959

Noel Coward's agent called about the Caesar role, but the studio is now discussing Fredric March.

NOVEMBER 1959

Adler talking about taking advantage of the Eady Plan for *Cleopatra*, which confirms London as headquarters.

Under the Eady Plan, it is possible for an American company to get financial aid from the British government if a certain percentage of cast and crew are British. The idea is to give more employment to British workers.

Mamoulian and I are to go to London to interview actors and look over facilities at Pinewood, Rank's studio. Bob Goldstein, in charge of Fox's operation in London and all of Europe, claims the facilities are excellent. I can't imagine, however, any location in England looking like Egypt, under any circumstances. And no one seems to have considered the weather.

— LONDON —

NOVEMBER 30, 1959

Saw Larry Olivier, who after much thought has decided against Caesar. He has played Shaw's *Caesar and Cleopatra* and Shakespeare's *Antony and Cleopatra*, and said frankly that he didn't think he could add to his luster by doing this motion picture. But I hope we can change his mind.

DECEMBER 2, 1959

Disaster! Nothing is right or as represented. Went to Pinewood with Mamoulian to see the facilities. It was rainy and cold, and Pinewood doesn't look like Egypt. In addition, the stages are small, and there are not enough of them.

The disappointment was so great that I became physically ill.

Meanwhile, Adler and Skouras had arrived to look over the Pinewood facilities. Despite my protests and Mamoulian's they are predisposed to accept the studio, because Skouras is trying to strengthen an association with Rank. There is always an angle in this business.

— NEW YORK —

DECEMBER 7, 1959

Went to see Elizabeth Taylor, who is convalescing from double pneumonia at Harkness Pavilion.

Her smallish room was crowded with flowers and piles of books. Liz looked well but was weak. She had had a severe bout. She's excited about the picture, enthusiastic that Oliver Messel will probably do her costumes. Had a painting of his on the wall, which she bought in London last year. She complained bitterly about the climate in New York. It occurred to me that if she is miserable and sick here, how will she be in England?

DECEMBER 8, 1959

Adler and Skouras back from Europe. Buddy flew from New York to Hollywood with me and told me of his "Christmas surprise" for me—he's bought an Italian version of *Cleopatra*, made by a producer named Lionello Santi, to keep it off the market. I pointed out that this adds another half-million dollars to our budget. But he is sure it's a good investment.

— HOLLYWOOD —

FEBRUARY 26, 1960

Had lunch with Adler, who expects the threatened Screen Actors Guild strike to last a long time. No telling when we can start the movie. He had just come from a meeting with Elizabeth's agents and feels we should find another Cleopatra.

"We'll never get together on a contract," he said. "Her demands are too great." I didn't feel Adler really wanted Elizabeth out, but the long sessions with agents and lawyers were beginning to wear him down. He said he was not feeling well. Or, perhaps he wants me to warn Frings not to be too tough. Buddy's mind often operates that way.

MARCH 7, 1960

Johnny Johnston and John DeCuir back from Turkey. A harrowing tale.

Skouras had an idea that we ought to attempt to shoot some of the exteriors for *Cleopatra* in Turkey and began negotiations with the Turkish Government. Johnny Johnston, a production manager, and John DeCuir, the art director, were elected to go and look for possible sites.

Turkish officials met them in Istanbul and took them to the Turkish Riviera, which they are anxious to develop. The government is willing to make any concession we ask, in exchange for our shooting there and bringing them not only business but publicity. According to Johnston, however, the garden spot of Turkey is so inaccessible, it would be impossible to shoot there on any practical basis. Living conditions and supplies were impossible. So Turkey is out as a location, but the cost of the trip is on our budget.

March 8, 1960

The Screen Actors Guild is on strike. Everyone at the studio is in a panic over what to do with *Cleopatra*. Skouras and Adler have now decided they want to make a co-production deal in Italy with Lionello Santi, who produced the Italian *Cleopatra*.

March 9, 1960

Mamoulian to Italy for a week to scout locations and look at studio space with Santi. Everyone at the studio seems enchanted with Santi.

March 14, 1960

The fight against my authority came out in the open this morning.

Schreiber called me into his office to tell me that Rouben, my art director John DeCuir, and production manager Johnny Johnston are going east tomorrow to meet with Sid Rogell, general manager of studio operations, Skouras, and the rest of the officials. He said it would not be necessary for me to go to New York as it was not planned to have me go to Italy.

"Why not?" I asked him.

"It has something to do with the Italian taxes," he said.

"Why can't I at least go to New York and discuss it with them? After all, it is my company's production."

"Walter, don't you understand? They don't want you."

I know something about Santi and I know Mamoulian, and this isn't going to work out. I settled for a wire to Buddy protesting his behavior, so I'd be on record, and decided to bide my time.

April 11, 1960

Another writer. We made a four-week deal for Lawrence Durrell to revise our script.

He is to receive $7,000 in Italian lire, and we are to pay his agents, Rosenberg-Coryell, the $700 commission. He is to start work on Friday, April 15, and deliver his revisions within four weeks. If we need additional revisions, he is to be paid at the rate of $2,500 a week in lire, with his agents' commission deducted and paid in dollars.

April 19, 1960

Received a memo from Mamoulian, who was now in London, on "making of *Cleopatra* in Italy." Not encouraging.

> Mamoulian noted:
>
> *There is a gulf between our way and the Italian way of making films intended for wide, popular consumption . . . the following seem to be the peculiarities of their modus operandi:*
>
> *Story construction is treated in a very free, loose manner . . . their whole approach to film making is much less demanding than ours. The talent and craftsmen involved seem to be easily satisfied with what we would consider unacceptable results. This attitude creates a real problem of semantics: Though they and we may use the same words, their meanings are different. For instance, what would there be referred to as a "great and perfect" location, would be called by us "limited and not suitable," and so on as applied to every facet of picture making. The whole standard of values and the criterion for achievement are widely different.*

After summing up the many difficulties likely to be encountered making a film in Italy, Rouben noted that it would be possible to "correct these unfavorable circumstances."

April 20, 1960

The romance with Santi is over. We are now to make the picture in England with locations in Italy.

In a full-page ad in *Variety*, Santi listed all of the pictures his Galatea Productions is involved in. Tucked between *The Story of Esther* and *The King Must Die* was "*Cleopatra* in color and for wide screen, directed by Rouben Mamoulian with Elizabeth Taylor." No mention of Fox. It looked as though *Cleopatra* was just one of his many productions.

Adler was furious. In no time at all the plans were changed once again. Goldstein, general manager of production in Europe, was told we would definitely be using Pinewood Studios.

April 28, 1960

Mamoulian back from Rome.

Rouben, who was supposed to be gone a week, stayed six.

— NEW YORK —

May 1, 1960

Had dinner with Elizabeth, Eddie, and Ketti Frings at the Colony in New York; discussed the *Cleopatra* situation.

We were all high about making the greatest picture ever. Elizabeth is especially excited about making a picture abroad. She wanted me to be sure and get Sidney Guilaroff as her hair stylist. He has done her hair on most of her pictures.

Sidney once worked at Bonwit Teller in New York. Then he went to Hollywood under contract to MGM and became a great favorite of many stars, especially Elizabeth and Ava Gardner, who always ask for him. Our only problem is to find out Sidney's availability and arrange to borrow him from MGM and get permission for him to work in London.

Our starting date is June 17.

— LONDON —

May 3, 1960

Nothing going right here.

Johnny Johnston and John DeCuir, who arrived here in advance, met me at the airport and insisted on a meeting at once to "take stock." The facilities at Pinewood, as anticipated, were not adequate; Denham Studio, which has the best stages in England, has been taken over by the U. S. Air Force and is not available; there was very little construction material available; we need a great many plasterers, and despite ads in the papers and on movie screens promising bonuses, we had less than a dozen. Of the dozens of draftsmen Goldstein said were available, we have been able to hire only a few, which makes it difficult to meet our starting date.

Additionally, there are basic differences between our ideas and methods and theirs. The English approach to film making is different from the American. The English can't be pushed. Although efficient, they don't want to work under pressure. We offered them bonuses which they refused. They would rather have their leisure at home and time to look after their gardens. Maybe they're right.

And they work differently. In America, a prop man goes out and finds things or rents them from places he knows about. They don't operate that way in England. First of all there are no props available for the *Cleopatra* period here, so everything has to be designed and then built, which means it will be expensive and slow.

We fear we may have a difficult time getting the proper results from the English extras, who are unfamiliar with the demands of this type of picture.

Also, it looks as though we are going to have trouble because of Sidney Guilaroff, the hairdresser. The British hairdressers' union is protesting his employment, claiming our using him is a reflection on the skill of the English hairdresser.

What worries us all most, however, is the weather. Even though this is spring, it is cold and damp, and Elizabeth is just over pneumonia.

May 6, 1960

Received a memo today from Adler saying the absolute limit on the *Cleopatra* budget is $4,000,000. Most unrealistic. We've spent half that already and haven't a foot of film.

May 9, 1960

David Merrick in town to try and get Laurence Olivier for *Becket*. We still hope to get him for *Cleopatra*, but we don't have a new script to show him, so I fear we may be out of the running. Caesar is a most difficult role to cast.

May 12, 1960

Bad news from Rome.

Bill Kirby, the English production manager, went with John DeCuir to Rome to check on the locations picked by Mamoulian. They also checked living accommodations and possibilities for renting filming equipment.

They found that the Olympic Games had taken over all the living space—something no one had considered. The studios Mamoulian chose need to be soundproofed, and it's doubtful that can be done in time. Also, there isn't the right kind of equipment available. A huge production like this needs a tremendous variety of lights, generators, and equipment. They have to be arranged for far in advance.

May 13, 1960

On the basis of yesterday's report, it has been decided to try and do everything possible in England if we can get Denham as Goldstein promised Adler. But the Denham Studio has been taken over by the U. S. Air Force. I called Jock Whitney, the

American ambassador, to ask if something could be worked out.

He was most co-operative and sympathetic, but after making every effort possible, he called back to say it was impossible.

WALTER WANGER

DORCHESTER HOTEL LONDON

DEAR WALTER TIME IS DRAWING NIGH ANYTHING NEW OF A HOUSE FOR A WIFE HUSBAND THREE CHILDREN AND ASSORTED ANIMALS STOP IMPERATIVE THAT MOST SATISFACTORY ACCOMMODATIONS BE FOUND STOP LOOKING FORWARD TO HEARING FROM YOU

YOUR SON EDDIE

MAY 14, 1960

Olivier is definitely out as Caesar.

He's going to do *Becket* for Merrick, so we are trying—against Skouras' wishes—to get Rex Harrison. Skouras told me there are two actors he doesn't want—Harrison and Richard Burton. He had Harrison in movies in the past, and they didn't do much at the box office; Burton had been in some great pictures, but Skouras doesn't think he means a thing at the box office.

Mamoulian arrived today—quite rightly furious. He wasn't met at the airplane and had to carry his own baggage. And he didn't have proper living accommodations. I am afraid he will be more upset when he gets a full report on our production problems.

Later the plans for the picture at this point were well summed up by Rouben Mamoulian in a 1300-word cable to Skouras. Rouben pointed out that the cuts the studio wanted made in our script would not merely shorten the picture but would change it so that it would not be the glamorous and colorful film we hoped to achieve.

Rouben also pointed out the difficulty of finding the right landscapes in England and the grave problem of weather conditions. He suggested we make the film in Italy and asked for a clear-cut decision as to where we are going, because the time left for preparation with limited labor is alarmingly and dangerously short.

May 19, 1960

This is absolute disaster.

Hollywood has given us an August 15 starting date, but we don't have enough studio space, don't have a full cast, don't have a script, and don't have a crew of laborers.

We need an enormous number of wigs, which are not available, and we don't have the costumes. The only positive note is the news that construction has started on the city of Alexandria at Pinewood. The workmen are on overtime. With luck the set will be ready in November—weeks after we are scheduled to use it.

May 27, 1960

Mr. Lew Schreiber
Twentieth Century-Fox Film Studios
Beverly Hills, California, U.S.A.

Dear Lew:

I talked to Elizabeth in New York last night. She was not too disappointed over Olivier not doing the picture because she always felt that he did not have any real enthusiasm for it. She is very anxious and excited over having Rex Harrison as Caesar . . . of all the available, established actors it seems to me, and I am sure Rouben agrees, that Harrison is the most capable and strongest talent available. I think you told me that you saw him play Henry VIII and how impressed you were. Not that this part is by any means similar, but he can handle costumes and he has strength and sex and, I think, will help Taylor enormously. The Sidney Guilaroff situation was brought up by Taylor last night. I explained to her that he could not work in the studio. She is insisting on bringing him over. I imagine any day you will be approached over a deal. I tried to ward off the situation by saying Oliver Messel wanted to control her hair problems in connection with the costumes, but she would not have any of it.

As always,
Walter Wanger

WALTER WANGER

DORCHESTER HOTEL LONDON

MUST CONFIRM SIDNEY GUILAROFF POSITION IMMEDIATELY OR HE WILL BE LOST AND THIS CANNOT HAPPEN

REGARDS

ELIZABETH

JUNE 2, 1960

Our first estimate on a foreign budget: $4,119,978.

It is not only totally unrealistic but it does not take into account any of the $2 million already spent.

— PARIS —

JUNE 3, 1960

Darryl F. Zanuck turns us down.

Mamoulian and I to Paris for the weekend to work with Lawrence Durrell and see Darryl Zanuck. He greeted us at the door of his apartment on the Left Bank. The walls were covered with very attractive pictures of Juliette Greco. Our purpose was to tell him of our serious trouble and try to get his help in putting the movie back on the rails, as he is one of the largest shareholders in Fox.

He took us to a superb dinner, then we went back to the apartment and discussed our problems. He isn't happy with the management but is having his own troubles. "There's nothing I can do at this time," he said, "and, please, don't even mention that you saw me here."

— LONDON —

JUNE 4, 1960

The budget was raised to $6,000,000 yesterday, dropped to $5,000,000 today. Also, the desert scenes are to be filmed in England. But instead of Cinemascope we are going to get Todd-AO!!!

Meanwhile the weather is terrible—cold, rainy, and cloudy, and the weather forecast is equally dismal. I called Elizabeth to tell her that the Italian locations are out. She was furious.

JUNE 13, 1960

Bob Goldstein called to say Elizabeth is planning to quit the picture.

Skouras telephoned from New York to say I am a saboteur and disloyal. He claims I had no right to tell Elizabeth that the Italian locations had been eliminated. Goldstein can't understand either why I didn't let Elizabeth start the picture, then tell her the Italian locations were out.

This hassle between us over the handling of Elizabeth has been brewing for some time. Every time Skouras sees Elizabeth in New York to discuss her contract—which she hasn't signed yet—he says something to infuriate her. The last time they met at her hotel, she told him she wouldn't make a deal with him. She wanted to deal with me. Skouras asked Elizabeth why she listened to "that old man." "Because he's honest," Elizabeth said.

JUNE 25, 1960

Skouras arrived today.

As always, Skouras was met at the airport by the film transportation man, who brought him two bottles of his favorite and unique Scotch and an envelope with English currency. Mamoulian and I met him at his suite in Claridge's, where he sat fiddling with his worry beads.

We presented him with a dossier compiled by his experts regarding the production, including a sheaf of weather reports on England for the past three years which indicated why the picture shouldn't be made here. "There's no sun," I said. "It's cold now, going to get colder. Elizabeth is liable to get pneumonia again."

"I don't believe in experts," Skouras shouted. "The weather is going to be fine. No one will get sick. England is the best place to make this picture. Go ahead. Shoot the picture."

Later, however, Rouben got a concession that we could go to Egypt for the desert shots.

JUNE 27, 1960

Skouras held a press conference about Fox plans today in the projection room of the Fox Soho Square headquarters. He was so tired he fell asleep three times—a fact the press duly noted.

JUNE 28, 1960

Met with Mamoulian on the script.

The first pages are not good enough to shoot. The sets are not nearly finished at Pinewood. They still can't get enough plasterers.

JULY 11, 1960
Buddy Adler died today in Hollywood of cancer. Despite our occasional differences on this picture, he was a good friend, and one has too few friends in this life. I am especially sad because he was so young.

JULY 13, 1960
Bob Goldstein is no longer head of European production. He is flying to Hollywood where he will run the studio there, succeeding Adler.

JULY 15, 1960
Sent a long memo to my lawyer in Hollywood.

Mr. Gregson Bautzer
Bautzer & Grant Attys.
190 North Canon Drive
Beverly Hills, California

Dear Greg:

I tried to reach you on the phone the other day to offer my sympathy because I know how upset you must be about the tragic passing of poor Buddy. Naturally, I am bewildered by the inexplicable turn of events that can cause such an early death, but what is there to say.

Regarding the material things in life, I started to write you a letter on July 5th, which I have rewritten after discussing the entire situation with Schwab, and I will try to make it as short as possible, but I am sure you can read between the lines. Naturally, I am very disturbed over the many delays and misadventures regarding *Cleopatra*. We certainly started out with a wonderful project that five stars wanted to do. After great difficulties, as you know, we had finally secured the services of Elizabeth Taylor and then we went after Olivier, who could have been signed up had the studio acted promptly enough. I am not going into all the details of how they kept operating without advising me of their activities when they sent Kurt Frings abroad to talk to Hepburn and to Elizabeth, nor am I going to belabor the point regarding the fact that Mamoulian and myself came to England November/December of 1959 and decided that would not be the ideal place to shoot the picture, but perhaps we might do the interiors provided we get a large enough stage. Then, on our return to America, we discovered that Skouras and everybody else was enchanted by Santi, and they suddenly decided to make the picture with Santi, and at that time they went over my head by sending Mamoulian, the art director, and the production manager Johnny Johnston to New York for conference with Rogell, Adler, and Skouras, telling me that they didn't want me there, I don't know for what reason, and they would be going for a week to Italy on a survey. DeCuir, Johnston, and Mamoulian were gone five weeks. On their return, the entire matter turned out to be a fiasco. They, Rogell and myself and Mamoulian proposed making the whole picture in Italy where it should have been made, and this was turned down in favor of an Eady Plan quota production whereby we shoot the interiors in London and the exteriors in Rome and the desert. Then came Adler's trip to Rome where, due to Goldstein's influence, he reversed himself and decided not to do anything in Rome because Goldstein had promised adequate stage space and workmen which, I said, were impossible to find, as you can see by the wires, and we were to do the entire picture in England. From then on, I think, the wires in the file that I had prepared for Skouras clarify the situation, with the exception of the fact that when Adler sent his congratulatory wire, it was implying that the plan was Goldstein's while it was Mamoulian's and my plan which we had to put over in opposition to Goldstein.

While they were in Rome with Santi, the budget arrived at was 5,200,000 dollars. Consequently, anybody could have figured out, by coming to England where they were shooting a five-day week instead of a six-day week, it must mount up to more. Also, we would be in two location operations—London and Rome—rather than just Rome, which again would run up expenses, especially under the Eady Plan, where we would have to take a lot of English staff wherever we went.

On June 2nd, we received a budget which was 6,000,000 dollars. This terrified Skouras and Adler, and Mamoulian and myself went off to Paris to work with Durrell, the writer; and I called him on the next day and was informed that the picture had to be cut to a $5,000,000 budget to be made entirely in England with the exception of maybe locations but not definitely, depending on the budget, and that the picture would be made in Todd-AO. This was done without consultation with Mamoulian and myself and we thought it was not only ridiculous but impossible.

Ever since May 20th we have been going around in circles, mostly due to the fact that Skouras and the Studio would refuse to read any reports, made not by Mamoulian and myself, but by the production staff hired by the Studio. Everyone connected with the picture has agreed that the cost in England would be greater than the cost anywhere else and also it is doubtful if the exteriors, even built here at great cost, could ever be shot because of the weather. If we are lucky and have an Indian summer, perhaps we can get this accomplished, but not with the quality that would be available elsewhere. Skouras has been here twice, as you know, and after meetings is still adamant in his insistence that the exteriors of Rome and Alexandria for *Cleopatra* will be shot in England. He is supported in his view by Bob Goldstein. They are, I am sure, doing this because they feel it would be cheaper and more efficient, although everyone on the production staff takes the opposite view, including every production executive that we have talked to over here. Even the English producers on small pictures go out of the country for exteriors to Spain, Italy, Germany, and France rather than attempting it here. Mamoulian and myself have not met one person who advocates shooting exteriors of this Mediterranean nature in England. We both feel it is our obligation to control the budget and we loathe to see an operation that is going to cost more and give less quality. As you know, one of the things promised Elizabeth when the deal was made was that the exteriors should be shot in Rome. Ever since I have been here, Goldstein and Skouras have been telling me that on account of the tax situation and the costs in Rome it would be impossible to go there. I know that they are exorbitant connected with American productions, but this isn't an American production; this is an English Eady Production on a quota basis and as far as they know there would be no problem if we went there for a few weeks. On this last trip, however, Skouras has agreed to a desert location for the picture in Egypt or any other available place so that we can now arrive at a decision for a proper location for the Alexandria and Rome shots. Although this has been promised, it has not been finalized. We must get these locations in order to make a good picture. I think it is essential and also would mean a great deal to Elizabeth, overcoming her objections to the way her picture has been handled. Another thing I am worried about is the weather here, which is not very good in the fall, as a matter of fact it has been terrible this summer and Elizabeth is so susceptible to colds and bronchitis that from the enclosed chart you will see what weather conditions are liable to be in September/October/November here and you know what the delays, due to her health, cost this production.

Incidentally, all of the things promised Adler by Goldstein have not been forthcoming:

1. The Denham Studio, which he said he would get, which would have enabled us to make our production more practical from the budget standpoint, was not obtained.
2. The proper number of draftsmen that are required to do this picture efficiently have never been available.
3. The plasterers that we need are nowhere to be seen and this is delaying the finishing of the sets.

As a matter of fact, the labor problem is so desperate here that the Rank Studios have put advertisements in the papers as well as putting slides on all the screens asking for plasterers to report. To date we have not received anything like the plasterers we need. Naturally, all of these delays and bonuses and promises to labor are going to run up the cost unnecessarily. In Italy, for instance, you can get 3—400 plasterers without any trouble. Here, we cannot get twenty!

I have tried to discuss these matters with Skouras. He refuses to listen to them. As a matter of fact, he wouldn't even discuss these matters.

What I really want you to understand is that Mamoulian and myself are very concerned with the practical and financial problems concerned with the picture far more than the heads of the organization, who pretend to be such excellent businessmen. There has been featherbedding in connection with the picture, where they have labor that they have promised weekend and overtime to, as you can see by the enclosed advertisement. They have given them things to do that we don't even need. The continual changes in the script have naturally held up the casting and the wardrobe and delayed preparing the picture properly, and the changes in the script have been due to the changes in budget from time to time. The thought that a picture of this type for Todd-AO could have been done on a limited budget—and 5 million dollars is limited when there have been the kind of expenses involved that have been involved in this—is something that is not too practical. I believe the picture eventually, with overtime and everything else, will exceed this, but I think that 6 million dollars would have been a far more reasonable budget to aim at than the four or five.

We are naturally trying to carry out our instructions, but they are very often contrary to the findings of professional producers or executives or directors.

I think if you get an opportunity to read the file I prepared for Skouras plus the enclosed, it will tell the story.

Both Rouben and myself are convinced that this project can still be put back on the track and be the biggest blockbuster and a great picture for the international market, properly made, and professionally produced. Confidentially, George Skouras was here this week and thinks of the picture, as properly made with a six-million-dollar budget, as a lush, exciting picture and that it can do a world's gross of 50 million dollars in Todd-AO. Spyros, on the other hand, argues with me that this picture has a ceiling of 20 million dollars, because it is not a biblical picture, and that it has a limited appeal to adults. I disagree violently with this point of view and I know that if it were done the way we planned, it would appeal to every female in the world from three to ninety! I could go on for days, but I hope Schwab will fill you in with the other details so you won't be bored with any more of my reports . . . This represents the joint thinking of

Mamoulian and myself and the reports of all the production minds available.

Best regards and
love to Dana, your
son, and yourself.
Walter Wanger

JULY 16, 1960

Bob Goldstein called from Hollywood to ask me to do a great favor for him: "Will you take over in my absence and run all of Europe for me?"

I said I'd do anything I could, under the circumstances.

Skouras, who was on the extension phone, said, "Walter, this is the greatest thing you have ever done in your life. I'll never forget it."

Within hours I started getting wires of congratulations from everybody at the studio. I'm glad to help, but suspect I'll have this job for no more than a month.

— ATHENS —

JULY 19, 1960

To Greece to meet Skouras in Athens. Then to Egypt to check on locations for *Cleopatra*.

Flying with Skouras is an adventure all by itself. When he gets on an airplane he talks to everybody—always fingering the worry beads. If there is a pretty woman aboard, he will go up to her and say, "You're very pretty. Are you married?" If the answer is yes, he will say, "What a lucky man your husband is."

He never gets to the plane until the last minute and has everybody in a nervous sweat all the time. One of his habits is to take a secretary from the office along in the car so he can dictate on his way to the airport. Invariably, however, he falls asleep and doesn't dictate a single line.

Tomorrow we go to Egypt where we will see Okasha, the Minister of Culture, and, hopefully, talk him into letting us shoot there.

— CAIRO —

JULY 20, 1960

Skouras is incredible.

Skouras is one of the most charming men in the world—when he wants to be. He seems to know everyone in the Egyptian government, and they love and respect him. At a big luncheon today he announced plans to make five pictures in Egypt, including *Salammbo*, starring Harry Belafonte and Gina Lollobrigida. He made it sound as though—thanks to him—Egypt would soon rival Rome as a world film center. The audience was enthusiastic.

Then he introduced me as Walter Wanger, who "will be in charge of all Fox operations in Europe, the Near and Middle East." That got a big hand too.

The last thing he did before we raced at seventy miles an hour for the plane was to arrange for the services of 10,000 men from the Egyptian Army to play the legions of Cleopatra. He also arranged for several locations in Egypt.

JULY 22, 1960

Extract from a letter from Patrick Barthropp, Ltd:

> Thank you for your inquiry with regard to a car for Miss Taylor from 8th August, 1960, for a period of sixteen weeks. We have pleasure in reserving the same Rolls-Royce Silver Cloud that she had last year, with the same chauffeur, Mr. Peter Bowden. . . .

JULY 27, 1960

Dear Rouben:

When the public buys tickets to see *Cleopatra*, they have every right to expect to see a great love story containing many passionate scenes between the most extraordinary people in history—Cleopatra, Caesar, and Antony. This is not in the shooting script and it is essential.

I am glad we are in agreement about this shooting script and I am sending you the following memorandum in the event that you wish to use it with Durrell.

I think some of his speeches are excellent and are of great value. However, for every good speech there have been injected more silly speeches than we have ever had in the script before. The elimination of these cozy, small-time sections of dialogue will help straighten out the shooting script in my opinion very much and should be done as soon as possible, even without Durrell.

The main facts and the important defects are the fact that the script is no longer attempting to be taut, suspenseful, melodramatic, or full of fast action. The whole canvas of this great world, with four dynamic personalities fighting for its domination, has been reduced to a bucolic, domestic, provincial picture of the nature of *Our Town*. The opportunity of using the greatest background of antiquity and shooting actually on the spot in Egypt gives us the opportunity to lift this picture to the great heights that are, in my opinion, obligatory.

To be precise, all of the scenes in the palace are completely without any sense of siege or feeling that the characters are prisoners in the palace and that there is doubt as to what is going to happen to our leading protagonists. It seems more like a nice weekend in Surrey where the water is going to be turned off. I still prefer the action and the impact in the potentials of the January 11th script as far as the great motion picture is concerned than I do this shooting script, although if the intent of the January 11th script can be injected into this shooting script, which I agree with you has better characterizations in many instances, we will get on the right track.

To be of service to us, Durrell must follow our plans rather than to try to reorganize the entire matter into a soft and unsuspenseful sonnet. The feeling of conspiracy, of distrust, of fast-acting spies, of life and death at great price is all lacking. There is plenty of material in the January 11th script that can be quickly put back and improve the script from the standpoint of making a successful motion picture. (For example, there is Taylor in such vital scenes as the establishment of the tremendous excitement of her achievement in presenting Caesar with a child named Caesarion, who becomes the hostage, in her mind, that is going to help her achieve her ambition to assume for him the throne of the world.) As a matter of fact, not even the name of Caesarion is established before Caesar's return to Rome. This is a vital thread in history and in the drama that must not be toyed with. Beyond that, it is essential that he be old enough to be reasonable in the last scenes. I do not believe that twelve years old, after a period of eighteen years, can be accepted by any intelligent picture-goer in 1961. I agree with you that the entrance into Rome is obligatory.

I also feel that with the Zoo, the third largest in the world, in Cairo, plus some ingenuity in picking locations, we could do this at a proper price without going overboard.

I think it is obligatory to establish the fact that Octavian clearly declared war on Cleopatra and not on Antony, and that in all the conferences prior to Actium, Cleopatra was the sore spot, just as she was instrumental by her activities in Rome in building toward Caesar's assassination. I agree with you, the scene between Antony and Cleopatra after the assassination of Caesar is unemotional and weak, again with the important points left out and the tremendous feeling of defeat that she must have felt, having been so close to success, is unemotional and unrewarding. Following this scene, there must be a thrilling exit from Rome.

I was most gratified last night that we are of one mind regarding these obligatory scenes and the type of dialogue that must be omitted in order to make the great motion picture that this subject matter offers. I feel our major error with Durrell was allowing him to deviate from improving actual scenes and trying to rewrite without sufficient experience in motion-picture scripts from start to finish. I have enormous faith in his talent, his ingenuity, and his ability to state things, but not in his ability to devise visual action with a beginning of a scene to a climax of a scene and a great curtain, all of which it is essential for you to have, so that we can fulfill our destiny with this tremendous project.

I also agree with you that your concept of Cleopatra is the correct one. A woman of many moods, of many emotions, turning off and on her hate, her ambition, her love, her excitement, and her dreams. At present, she could be a placid heiress, living on a big estate in the British countryside, rather than the unique and most fascinating woman in the world with ambition to rule the world with Caesar and then to place her great son, Caesarion, on the throne as King of the World. The always-present spying, treacherous killing, dramatic Sword of Damocles over the existence of all the characters, the fantastic marriages for power, the deals, the accepted intrigue and suspicion which were indicated in the January 11th script, have been vacuumed out of this with weekend charades and silly sayings.

Excuse the continuity of the memorandum and the English, which is not Elizabethan, but it has been dictated by a very concerned producer at five o'clock in the morning. As I am going to New York in connection with the script and the deal with Taylor, I am writing this memorandum so that I can present our ultimate concept to her as clearly and forcefully as possible. I know that the Egyptian potential gives us a chance that has never been done on the screen before. I hope we can have another meeting before I leave.

With every good wish, as always,
Yours,
Walter Wanger

— NEW YORK —

JULY 28, 1960

Elizabeth had refused to sign her contract so Goldstein ordered me to go to New York to "get her" to do it.

I met Schreiber, who had come from California just for this, at my hotel. He was in a sweat, certain we'd never get her to sign, particularly since the starting date had been pushed back again, and we wanted a further extension of time from her. The new starting date is September 25.

At the Park Lane, Elizabeth was lovely in a negligee, no make-up, demonstratively affectionate with Eddie in the living room. She was well aware of the turmoil she was causing with Skouras and Schreiber.

She told me the contract was fine, gave me the delay in starting I requested, and suggested we look at Peter Finch for Caesar. She promised to sign the contract later in the afternoon but told me to tell Skouras she was "still looking it over" to keep him on edge a little while longer.

While I was having dinner at the Colony, the contract was delivered to me as promised. I called Skouras instantly. "Walter, you are a miracle man," he said, "How did you do it? I'll never forget it." I told him Elizabeth couldn't have been nicer about the whole thing.

In my room that night I read her contract, from Elizabeth's point of view. If the picture runs over schedule a few months, as I suspect it must, she stands to make two or three million dollars.

Some of the highlights of the contract were:

Salary of $125,000 for sixteen weeks' work.

$50,000 per week after sixteen weeks.

10% of the gross income of the movie.

In addition, there was page after page of special conditions:

In lieu of reimbursing the Artist for her expenses in connection with her services hereunder, the Corporation shall pay the Artist the sum of Three Thousand Dollars ($3,000.00) per week for all living expenses, including food and lodging, while she is rendering her services hereunder, commencing on the date the Artist reports to the Corporation in London, England, or such other place as may be designated by the Corporation, until the Artist completes her said services. . . .

The Corporation shall pay the cost of first-class, round-trip transportation from Los Angeles, California, to London, England, or such other place as may be designated by the Corporation, for four (4) adults including the Artist, and three (3) children . . .

In the event that the Artist desires to consult with her agent, Kurt Frings, in reference to her services in connection with the picture contemplated herein, while she is rendering her services on location hereunder, and if said agent deems it necessary that he consult with the Artist, the Corporation shall pay the first-class, round-trip transportation of said agent from Los Angeles, California, to such location, and the incidental expenses of said agent in connection with such trip; provided, however, that the obligation of the Corporation under this paragraph shall be limited to one (1) such round trip to such location.

She even got the promise of a 16 mm. print of the completed film for her personal use.

— LONDON —

AUGUST 20, 1960

Just received a construction report on the city of Alexandria and the other sets, which will cover eight acres.

According to the report, we have 142 miles of tubular steel; enough RR ties for four miles of track; 20,000 cubic feet of timber; seven tons of nails; 300 gallons of paint—in short, enough construction material for a development of about forty houses.

Rental for just the iron scaffolding supporting Cleopatra's palace is costing us $2,000 a week.

The palm trees were imported from Hollywood; the fresh palm fronds are flown in from Egypt and Nice. I am told that hundreds of swallows roost in the palms at night. They must think they have already reached the Mediterranean.

A trail of spoiled fish was laid down in order to entice sea gulls away from a nearby gravel pit.

Cleopatra's palace at Alexandria covers twenty acres, of which four acres are under water resting on 15,000 railroad ties supporting marbleized gold, gilt buildings. Cleopatra's white marble palace on top of the railroad ties is the most remarkable set ever built in England. The interior is almost as large and twice as high as Grand Central Station.

Four large sphinxes, 52 feet high and 65 feet wide are being constructed.

August 23, 1960

MR AND MRS EDDIE FISHER

FIRST CLASS PASSENGERS

SS LEONARDO DA VINCI

EN ROUTE TO NAPLES

HAVE LARGE CORNER SUITE AT DORCHESTER AND BATHROOM DRESSING ROOM LIVING ROOM FOR YOU AND EDDIE ADJOINING TWO DOUBLE BEDROOMS AND TWO BATHROOMS AND SITTING ROOM FOR NURSE AND CHILDREN FORTY THREE POUNDS A DAY STOP YOU CAN HAVE IT TEMPORARY OR PERMANENTLY STOP CHILDRENS SUITE AS OF TWENTY FIFTH AND YOUR SUITE AS OF THIRTY FIRST AUGUST

PLEASE CONFIRM

LOVE TO YOU BOTH

WALTER

August 24, 1960

LEW SCHREIBER

CENTFOX

LOS ANGELES

DEAR LEW GUILAROFF CALLED ME TWICE FIRST TIME TO TELL ME COULDNT GET HERE BEFORE SATURDAY AND I ADVISED HIM WE HAD ORDERED WIGS AND WERE UNDERWAY AS WE COULD NOT WAIT FOR HIM SECONDLY MADE IT CLEAR THAT HE WOULD NOT BE ALLOWED ON SET BUT COULD WORK WITH ELIZABETH AT HOTEL AND I COULD GUARANTEE HIM NOTHING REGARDING ANY LESSENING OF REGULATIONS HERE BUT THOUGHT HE SHOULD GET ON WITH MESSEL AND HAIRDRESSERS HE AGAIN CALLED ME NEXT DAY AND SAID HE WAS WORRIED MAYBE HE SHOULDNT COME IF

HE COULDNT OPERATE AS HE WAS ACCUSTOMED TO I ASSURED HIM THAT I WOULD DO EVERYTHING I COULD PERSONALLY TO MAKE THINGS WORK BUT AGAIN MADE IT CLEAR I COULD NOT UPSET THE REGULATIONS HERE AND THAT MUST BE UNDERSTOOD I DONT KNOW WHAT HE MEANS BY MY TAKING CARE OF HIM I SIMPLY SAID I WOULD DO WHAT I COULD TO MAKE THINGS WORK AND IF THEY DIDNT HE COULD WITHDRAW FROM THE PICTURE I DONT SEE WHY WE SHOULD GIVE HIM A GUARANTEE IF THE SETUP WORKS HE WILL REMAIN AS ELIZABETH WANTS HIM AND IF HE IS NOT ABLE TO FUNCTION THIS NOT OUR FAULT I TOLD HIM I THOUGHT IT DEPENDED ON HOW HE HANDLED THE SITUATION HIMSELF CONFIDENTIALLY I FEEL IF HE DOESNT STEP ON OTHER PEOPLES TOES HE MIGHT BE HELPFUL TO ELIZABETH BUT IF HE ATTEMPTS TO EXERT TOO MUCH INFLUENCE IT MIGHT BE RESENTED BY THE PEOPLE HERE.

REGARDS
WALTER

AUGUST 31, 1960

Liz and Eddie arrive in London from Naples.

Their arrival at the airport was a scene out of *La Dolce Vita* with newsmen and photographers swarming like honeybees. I got Liz and Eddie away from the crowd via a rear exit without incident. But at the Dorchester the press set up an angry clamor.

Elizabeth refused to see them or pose for pictures because of the harsh way she had been treated in London last year during *Suddenly Last Summer*. Some of the newsmen waiting outside her suite told me they intended to boycott Liz and the picture. When I relayed their comments to Liz she shrugged and said nothing would induce her to make an appearance or allow them to photograph her. I must say she has a lot of courage. There are very few actresses with nerve enough to stand up to the British press.

SEPTEMBER 6, 1960

I am no longer head of European production.

Sid Rogell came through London on his way to Greece. He asked me about the *Cleopatra* script, and I gave it to him and told him of some of our problems. He was living at the Savoy where he bumped into Darryl Zanuck over from Paris on business, who was also staying there. Rogell apparently showed the script to Darryl, who didn't like it. Darryl apparently called Skouras to report on what he thought was wrong.

Skouras called me back and said, "Jesus Christ, Walter! At your age, you ought to know better than to talk to a fellow like Rogell."

I said I had been advised I was to look after Rogell while he was in London.

"Well, you ought to know better," said Skouras. "Just for that I don't want you to have anything to do with Europe. You just stick to *Cleopatra*."

SEPTEMBER 26, 1960

I hear Skouras is putting Sid Rogell in charge of Europe, as of today.

BOOK II

FIASCO IN LONDON

[1960–1961]

— LONDON —

SEPTEMBER 29, 1960
A bad beginning.

SIR TOM O BRIEN
17 WATERLOO PLACE
LONDON W1

DEAR TOM SEVERAL DAYS AGO YOU ASSURED ME THAT YOU HAD IN HAND THE PROBLEM CONCERNING SIDNEY GUILAROFFS WORK ON THE PICTURE STOP AS YOU KNOW WE HAD TWO STOPPAGES OF WORK BY THE HAIRDRESSING DEPARTMENT YESTERDAY OUR FIRST DAY OF SHOOTING STOP YOU WERE VERY DEFINITE THAT THE SITUATION MUST BE RESOLVED BECAUSE THE ENTERPRISE WAS MOST IMPORTANT AND FOR ME NOT TO WORRY STOP AS YOU ADVISED APPLICATION FOR WORK PERMIT HAS BEEN LODGED AND A REQUEST FOR A MEETING BETWEEN THE UNION AND THE BFPA HAS BEEN MADE STOP I AM DEEPLY CONCERNED BECAUSE I HAVE NOT BEEN ABLE TO REACH YOU NOR HAVE I HAD ANY COMMUNICATION FROM YOU EXCEPT THAT YOUR SECRETARIES ASSURED ME THAT THEY HAD GIVEN YOU MY MESSAGES STOP REPRESENTING FOX WE ARE FACING A VERY SERIOUS ECONOMIC CRISIS IF THIS MATTER IS NOT STRAIGHTENED OUT IMMEDIATELY AS YOU PROMISED STOP IT WILL FORCE THE COMPANY TO SHUT DOWN AND WHAT THE RESULTS WILL BE BEYOND THAT I DREAD TO THINK STOP YOU HAVE BEEN APPRISED OF

THE SERIOUSNESS OF THE SITUATION BY OUR EXECUTIVES IN LOS ANGELES AS WELL AS HERE AND I HOPE YOU WILL BE ABLE TO IMMEDIATELY REMEDY THE SITUATION AS AGREED STOP I CANNOT OVEREMPHASIZE HOW IMPORTANT THIS IS TO OUR COMPANY AND THE INDUSTRY

REGARDS
WALTER WANGER

Letter to Solly Wurtzel, associate production manager on *Cleopatra* and my assistant.

Dear Solly:

Please advise me whether our insurance covers Elizabeth Taylor not reporting today on account of a sore throat.

September 30, 1960

Liz has a cold. We started shooting around her. Two minutes and 20 seconds of sunshine. Temperature: 45 degrees.

Since there are many scenes in the film that do not require Liz, we started on an exterior shot which the art department had been preparing for some time. The scene of Caesar (Peter Finch) and Mark Antony (Stephen Boyd) entering the city of Alexandria, peopled by thousands of extras, was a "glass shot."

The camera and crew were mounted on a high platform opposite the impressive set—a million dollars' worth of temples, other buildings, and the bow of a large galley, floating in a tank. In front of the camera lens there was a glass on which had been painted an Egyptian countryside and buildings. These appeared to extend out from the real set, substituting for the drab British countryside. When done skillfully, it is impossible to tell what is real scenery and what is painted on the glass. However, the light on the real set and that painted on the glass must match exactly during shooting, which makes it tricky.

The hairdressers' union is still adamant about letting Guilaroff work in England. Officially, it takes the position that by the London office's failure to get a work permit for Guilaroff we are forcing Guilaroff down their throats. And by using him we are casting aspersions on the art of hairdressing as practiced in England.

Their real antagonism stems from the fact that Guilaroff didn't get along with some of the female members of the union the last time he worked in England. They vowed then that he would never get another special work permit.

OCTOBER 2, 1960

Elizabeth still ill. Dr. Carl Heinz Goldman, a leading Harley Street physician, attending her.

Still having problems with the script.

Met this evening with Sir Tom O'Brien, Member of Parliament and head of the British Motion Picture Producers' Association, about Guilaroff. Sir Tom is a great character; jovial, a stout-drinker and an old friend. He wants to do everything possible to help us but says his hands are tied. This silly situation is getting desperate.

Speaking for myself, I can do without Guilaroff, who considers himself an authority on everything from hair to scripts and production, probably because he is paid like an executive—$1,100 a week plus $600 a week expenses.

OCTOBER 3, 1960

Two minutes and 15 seconds of sunshine today. It's bitter cold. Elizabeth has a temperature of 100 degrees and can't come to the studio for wardrobe tests.

Oliver Messel, the costume designer, is complaining about his position and authority; Sidney Guilaroff is complaining about his position; Mamoulian is complaining about the writers; Skouras called Rogell to complain about Mamoulian.

OCTOBER 5, 1960

Skouras cabled, indignantly denying he made any attack against me to Elizabeth. Added he was "worried to death" about our script, urged me to avoid friction and delays, produce a great picture.

To which I can only say, "Let's get on with it."

OCTOBER 8, 1960

Skouras called Rogell and told him he should get close to Liz and Eddie; he should play golf with Eddie and send flowers to Liz. Rogell told me of the conversation and said that he will wait for me to introduce him to them before beginning to try and win them over. Later in the day, however, Eddie called to tell me that Rogell phoned to ask about Elizabeth's health.

Everybody is trying to play Liz. The Fox people believe I am using her too, but the fact is she and I are not as close as they think. I am not a member of her inner circle. I have always kept what I consider to be a proper professional relationship. I am not a sycophant or a hanger-on, which is why I think Liz respects our relationship, which has been a wonderful one as far as I am concerned.

OCTOBER 10, 1960

Went to Elizabeth's suite at the Dorchester to say goodbye to Eddie, who is going to New York for a few days.

Guilaroff was there discussing her hair, and Oliver Messel was attempting a fitting. Each man had assistants and they had their assistants. It was a scene of mass confusion.

But Elizabeth was in tears. She didn't want Eddie to leave. She kissed and hugged him before he left the room. When he left she ran to the room telephone again to have him paged in the lobby. She told him on the telephone again to be careful and hurry back. She said she was planning to stay up all night until he called her from California.

OCTOBER 11, 1960

Meeting tonight with the entire membership of the English Motion Picture Producers' Association. The subject: Sidney Guilaroff. This is ridiculous. The Cold War continues, and we are all casualties.

TELEGRAM TO SIR TOM O'BRIEN:

DEAR TOM I CANNOT IMPRESS TOO STRONGLY ON YOU THE SERIOUS POSITION WE FIND OURSELVES IN THAT WITH THE RESIGNATION OF THE HAIRDRESSERS AND THE IMPOSSIBILITY OF GETTING REPLACEMENTS FROM YOUR ORGANIZATION THAT OUR CORPORATION IS BEING PUT IN AN UNTENABLE POSITION BECAUSE WE HAVE HAD TO SUSPEND OPERATIONS AND CONTINUE TO CARRY ON OUR PAYROLL AN ENORMOUS OVERHEAD STOP NATKE MUST IMMEDIATELY SUPPLY US WITH SUITABLE HAIRDRESSERS OR WE WILL HAVE TO CLOSE DOWN PERMANENTLY STOP EVERY HOUR COUNTS AS THE COMPANY CANNOT UNDERSTAND THE DAY TO DAY DELAY IN FINDING THESE SUITABLE HAIRDRESSERS FROM NATKE PLEASE CONTACT ME AT THE STUDIO OR AT HOME

REGARDS
WALTER WANGER

OCTOBER 12, 1960

Met with Elizabeth at the Dorchester about the Guilaroff situation.

Liz still had a low fever, but she hoped to be well within a day or two. I told her the situation—that if Guilaroff continued on the picture we would be faced with another expensive hairdressers' walkout.

"I don't want the picture to close down," she said. "I don't want a strike, but I don't want Oliver Messel to do my hair." Messel, who was designing Elizabeth's wardrobe, had said he couldn't prepare her properly as Cleopatra unless he also designed her jewelry, shoes, hairdress, wigs, etc.

"Whatever you work out is all right with me," Liz finally conceded. As usual, she couldn't have been nicer.

October 13, 1960

The London *Daily Mail* has a story out that Liz has not been appearing in public because she is too fat. The Fox press department issued a denial. The *Express* also denied the story—said she is ill and not overweight.

October 14, 1960

Heavy frost. Two-minutes, 15 seconds of sunshine, one thousand extras. Liz still ill.

October 15, 1960

Sir Tom O'Brien called and complained that the union is embarrassed by the deal I made with the hairdressers, but he is happy they are back at work.

I had promised the girls a bonus if they would go back to work—anything to get on with the action, and the hell with protocol.

Mamoulian called Skouras, who was all kindness but can't understand why we don't shut down the company and let the insurance carry the burden. Rogell, on the other hand, believes we should make every effort to continue shooting around Elizabeth, who still has a temperature.

October 18, 1960

Trouble brewing with the insurance companies.

F. G. Geddes, the insurance adjuster for Topliss & Harding representing Lloyd's of London, is on the set every day checking everything we are doing. He knows everything that is going on.

Whenever anyone doesn't show up, or if a horse breaks a leg, or a piece of equipment is lost or stolen, Geddes is right on it. He is savvy enough about movies to be able to make suggestions to the production department on scenes they can shoot without Liz, so the picture continues.

Received a copy of a memo to Geddes from Lord Evans, the Queen's physician, who was called in as a consultant by Dr. Goldman.

He traced Elizabeth's illness back to an abscess she had three weeks ago. Then she developed what seemed to be a common cold, but it was accompanied by a mild fever which persisted despite treatment with a variety of antibiotics. He cautiously diagnosed it as "a case of infection of doubtful origin."

He said it could be a virus or some sort of a Bacillus abortus or Malta fever infection.

Whatever the cause, he pronounced her clearly unfit for work and ordered her to stay in bed until the fever subsided.

October 20, 1960

Mamoulian getting unhappy.

Rogell is an outspoken man whose first loyalty is to Twentieth. A company man, he didn't think Rouben was working out for us, and he didn't hesitate to say so.

Rouben is an Armenian who is very set in his ways but he has great integrity. He cannot tolerate not knowing what is going on, he doesn't like interference, and he doesn't like to be "pushed" as Rogell is "pushing" him. He takes great pride in his artistry. Like many directors, he fancies himself an expert on the entire art of cinema. He considers himself a writer, thinks he knows more about the camera than the cameraman—and is not always tactful about speaking out. Even in the tension of this situation which requires 24-hour-a-day attention, he refuses to discuss business at mealtimes. He frequently tried my patience, but I believe in his artistry and am willing to let him find his own level.

In the evening went to the theater with Liz and Eddie to see *The Millionairess*.

Liz is well aware of the fact that even with the extra time provided by her illness we still aren't organized. She has been around too long not to be aware when a company is muddling—and we are muddling. She is getting tired of the press laying the blame for our confusion on her. She is especially irked that Skouras is using her as the scapegoat with the insurance company.

OCTOBER 21, 1960

The doctors think Elizabeth will not be ready for work until November 1. The insurance company wants us to issue suspension notices to all the other members of the cast and close down the picture.

Skouras is in town. The main issue in his mind seems to be discovering how much of our losses can be recovered by insurance. Looks like a battle brewing between the insurance companies and Skouras.

Skouras saw some of the rushes with Peter Finch and Stephen Boyd. He doesn't think Finch has enough dignity and strength or power to play Caesar. Part of this he blames on Mamoulian and me. He says we don't seem to be handling the cast with enough authority. "I don't care for what I've seen or what I've heard," Skouras said. Mamoulian, naturally, is very upset.

We are still shooting around Liz and doing everything we can, building special sets, rushing sets in and tearing them down, in order to get moving. So far we are not ready for Liz anyway; the costumes are not completed and the script is still not right. All the scenes shot up to now are exteriors—nothing in which the actors have any important dialogue. We are just setting the stage for the big scenes.

OCTOBER 22, 1960

Big session on insurance at the 20th Century-Fox headquarters in Soho Square.

The insurance company wants us to close down and recast Elizabeth; Skouras wants to collect the insurance and start over again; Rogell wants to keep going ahead in the hope that Elizabeth will soon be well enough to work.

The weather is terrible; cold, rainy, and damp.

OCTOBER 24, 1960

Another meeting with all the executives at which Ernie Holding, the Fox production executive, estimated that our loss since September 29 has been $121,428 a day. The loss to date: over two million dollars.

Skouras decided to trim the budget to five million dollars and readjust the shooting schedule from 95 to 75 days. At the same time he announced that I am in charge of making the picture on the new schedule and budget. Every time he comes to Europe he gives someone else complete authority, but the fact is he keeps the power for final decision to himself. Anyway, the new budget and schedule are impossible—we've spent almost half the budget already. But Skouras, as usual, won't listen to facts.

"Make it," he said.

OCTOBER 26, 1960

Skouras continues his usual routine of "You're the producer, no alibis, you're too nice." He claims I am responsible for the delays because I insisted on having Liz.

"You're such a stubborn sonofabitch," he said. "You've ruined us by having that girl in the picture. We'll never finish the picture with her. I wish to hell we'd done it with Joanne Woodward or Susan Hayward—we'd be making money now."

I told Skouras I thought Liz was going to be great. Then I mentioned that I had just talked with Harold Mirisch in Los Angeles, who said he just called off his deal with Liz for *Irma La Douce* and *Two for the Seesaw*, so she was free now.

"I authorize you to sign Liz for two more pictures—at once," Skouras said without missing a beat!

Heavy fog makes shooting impossible. We had called five hundred extras, and could hardly find them on the set in the fog.

OCTOBER 29, 1960

Liz taken to the London Clinic.

Talked with the doctors to find out what is really the trouble. One of them told me she has Malta fever—a tenacious bug that's as hard to shake as it is to diagnose.

"Convalescence is usually tedious—at least three months," the doctor said.

I hope he's wrong—for Elizabeth's sake as well as ours.

NOVEMBER 2, 1960

London *Daily Mirror* called me to check on whether we are going to replace Liz. "No Liz, no Cleo," I said.

Met with Geddes and Rogell all afternoon. The insurance company wants us to recast the picture with another actress.

They gave us a list of the actresses they felt could play Cleopatra: Audrey Hepburn, Marilyn Monroe, Rosanna Podesta, Kim Novak, Shirley MacLaine, Sophia Loren and Gina Lollobrigida. We pointed out that no other actress has sufficient drawing power. We want Liz because our first objective is a great picture, and Liz is essential for that.

Mamoulian called to complain about Rogell hurrying and harassing him. Rogell called to say Mamoulian didn't seem concerned enough about our situation. I tried to pacify both of them.

We are all under great tension. Our problems inevitably end up on the front pages. Meanwhile, Liz is still in the clinic. Dr. Goldman assured me that she will be fine in a few days, but the weather is miserable, which means we can't shoot any exteriors.

Mamoulian is unhappy with the script, and Skouras is clamoring to cancel shooting, while the insurance company is still insisting that we find a replacement. To top it all off, the ridiculous Guilaroff situation is not yet near resolution.

Since I've had my heart attacks I learned not to get excited—the only person I hurt is myself. I've trained myself to take things in stride, and on this production I anticipated many of our problems: the bad weather, Elizabeth's illness, our inability to get proper space and people. So I was prepared.

NOVEMBER 7, 1960

The doctors were wrong. Liz really had a virus infection. She was dismissed from the clinic this morning.

Geddes telephoned me, very upset. He just heard Liz had left the hospital and returned to the Dorchester Hotel without the sanction of the insurance company's doctors. I checked with Dr. Goldman who said Liz was permitted to leave the hospital after consultation with Lord Evans and himself.

NOVEMBER 8, 1960

An hour wasted over another ridiculous and undignified detail: the boil Liz had. Rogell forwarded a letter from our indefatigable insurance man, Geddes, who wants a statement from me or Dr. Goldman or anyone else concerning Elizabeth's "illness," which he described as a "boil on the buttocks" during the period September 25 to September 29.

Excerpt from my letter to Geddes:

> On September 26 she again had fittings and at eleven o'clock that night she went to the Dominion Theatre to see rushes of her tests with her husband, Eddie Fisher, and myself. She laughingly said she had a small boil on one buttock, or something of the sort, but in no way did it impair her from standing for fittings. From her behavior it was clear to me that it was not causing her any distress.

November 9, 1960

Mamoulian called this morning to say his dinner appointment with Liz was called off because she isn't feeling well.

He said he didn't like the sound of it so I called Liz's apartment at the Dorchester. A woman's voice whispered, "Mrs. Fisher will call back later." Late in the afternoon a reporter from the *Daily Mail* called to say Liz had been taken to the clinic on a stretcher. I called Eddie at the clinic. He was too upset to talk other than to say Liz is under sedation and Lord Evans, Dr. Goldman, and a neurologist are in attendance.

A few minutes later the *Daily Express* called to say Liz has meningitis. I called Dr. Goldman, who said she had a terrible headache but not meningitis. I called the *Express* back to deny the meningitis rumor.

Eddie phoned back weeping and frightened. He called Dr. Rex Kennamer in Hollywood who is flying right over. Dr. Goldman called to say Liz is much better. "Probably an infected tooth," he said.

November 14, 1960

The insurance company offered Skouras $1,750,000 and promised to reinsure Elizabeth.

He wants more. The offer was presented by David Metcalf who was one of the junior partners in the firm that carried our insurance. He is the son of an old friend, Major Metcalf, who was aide-de-camp to the Prince of Wales when I knew him.

November 17, 1960

Eddie Fisher says Skouras is going to close down the picture and go on with it later, but told Eddie not to tell me. Sid Rogell said Skouras told him to tell Mamoulian and myself we'd better get ready to go back to Los Angeles, but not to quote him. Tom O'Brien has heard rumors we are going to close down and he wants to know what to tell his labor people.

NOVEMBER 18, 1960

There is nothing more we can shoot without Liz. We must come to a stop.

In the morning Rouben and I met with the Works Committee at the studio to explain why it was necessary for us to give the workers notice. They were very understanding.

In the afternoon we went on the Alexandria set and told the workers from the camera platform through loudspeakers we were shutting down. We said that we planned to resume filming as soon as Elizabeth was well enough.

NOVEMBER 21, 1960

Skouras arrived today and told the press that *Cleopatra* will be completed. He said that Liz is the perfect Cleopatra. "We cannot abandon her just because she has been ill," he said.

Skouras told me that when the picture resumes it will still be on the Eady Plan and done between London and Egypt. This seems final.

NOVEMBER 25, 1960

Geddes drops a bombshell.

The insurance people are contending that Elizabeth made a serious omission in her statement to them—thereby invalidating her insurance. They have found that on September 14, Elizabeth received "urgent medical treatment" from a doctor, which she neglected to mention in her medical statement.

Eddie tells me that this is what happened: Elizabeth was unable to sleep and was having palpitations. She called the hotel doctor, who was not available, so an outside doctor was sent up to examine her.

This doctor said that Elizabeth had a heart flutter, which he described as tachycardia. She believed it was only her nerves and, never having had a heart condition and not knowing the doctor, she ignored what he said and took the sedation he gave her. She apparently either forgot the incident or discounted it in filling out a long insurance form. The insurance company claims that her answers were inaccurate. That's their loophole. But Dr. Goldman says her answers were correct.

DECEMBER 9, 1960

Received our new starting date: January 3, in London. Liz and Eddie are to return December 23.

Rogell and DeCuir back from Egypt checking on locations. Their report is good.

Skouras and Goldstein in their anxiety to get the script finished asked Nunnally Johnson, who was in London, to work on it. Rouben has his own writer, Marc Brandel, who has also been working on the script all along; Rouben was not sold on the idea that Johnson was the right man to succeed Brandel. But this was one of Skouras' and Goldstein's impulsive telephone decisions. The studio's commitment to Johnson is $140,000.

DECEMBER 28, 1960

Another wasted day.

Elizabeth came back to town looking much better and prepared to work. She showed up at the studio early this morning to make herself up and get ready for tests. But it was impossible to go on the stages. The studio failed to turn on the heat last night, and Liz had to wait until the afternoon before the stage was warm enough to make tests.

NEW YEAR'S EVE

I asked Liz and Eddie to join me for New Year's Eve. We went out to dinner with the Mamoulians and my daughter Steffi, who was in town on a holiday. The restaurant was packed with all the theatrical and cafe society set, but it wasn't too gay.

Our waiter was so overawed by Elizabeth that he kept making remarks and sneaking a drink or two on the side. It ended up by his spilling coffee all over Liz's brand new Dior dress, which had just arrived by air from Paris that afternoon. Liz took it very nicely—smiled and said it was an accident. She went home to change. Then we all went to two or three other night clubs where we were joined by Sidney Guilaroff and others.

The Guilaroff situation at the studio is still the same. The hairdressers say they will walk out if he comes on the set, so he visits Liz at her hotel and fixes her hair for tests in her dressing room.

JANUARY 3, 1961

Mamoulian does not seem interested in conferring with Johnson over the script because he still didn't think he is the right choice.

The interplay of personalities, while no more complex than it usually is in the business, is holding up our chances of getting the picture before the cameras. Mamoulian is unhappy with Nunnally Johnson's approach to the script and Nunnally, who is aware of Rouben's feelings, is unhappy over that. As usual, I am in the middle as arbiter. Liz doesn't like the Johnson material or the old script. She and Eddie suggested Paddy Chayefsky to do a rewrite, and Eddie is talking about making the film in Hollywood, as he too is fearful of the climate here and Elizabeth's health.

JANUARY 4, 1961

Paddy Chayefsky sent a very interesting letter about his views on the script, but they would require six months for the rewrite. We don't have the time.

Almost had the Guilaroff situation settled.

I made another side deal with the lady hairdressers—a promise of a bonus—after convincing them that Guilaroff was not as arrogant as they believed him to be. Then, as luck would have it, Guilaroff went to see Liz in her dressing room followed by one of the lady hairdressers. Either the wind or Guilaroff slammed the door in her face. The hairdresser said it was Guilaroff. So the hassle is back on full blast.

We are not starting Monday, as we should, because the script is not satisfactory. Liz has just advised me she has chills and can't shoot tests tomorrow.

January 5, 1961

Skouras offers the insurance company a deal. He suggests that they pay $3,750,000 in settlement of the present loss, with Fox to pay the underwriters 20 per cent of the profits on *Cleopatra* up to $2,000,000. Alternately, the company can pay $2,250,000 in settlement of the present loss with no share of the profits. In addition, the company has to agree to renew cast insurance to Elizabeth and the other principals.

To sweeten the pot he pointed out that if the insurance company accepts either of his offers they will avoid lots of bad publicity and the cost of legal action. If they accept his first offer and *Cleopatra* is a big box-office success, they will suffer only a relatively small loss.

January 6, 1961

Went to see Liz and Eddie at the Dorchester for a conference.

They live like royalty with children, dogs, cats, retainers, and supplicants for favor all over the place. Writers and famous people are always dropping in.

Liz and Eddie are constantly taking on projects, and the phone rings continually, with friends or agents calling in from Hollywood or Switzerland or Rome. The order of the day is—deals. Liz is enthusiastically interested in everything and anything, especially films and the theater. She has enough knowledge about show business to edit *Variety* with her left hand.

January 10, 1961

Script problems.

Liz and Peter Finch said the scene they were rehearsing was unplayable. Mamoulian, however, had approved it, even though I am sure he didn't consider it perfect. But he did want to get on with the picture and thought he would get something out of the scene on the set.

Liz said she wanted to see me later at the Dorchester for a script conference. She was in bed, not feeling well, when I arrived with Rogell. Liz said she was not happy with the script and insisted we call Skouras from her room. She managed to upset Skouras too.

Rogell suggested to me later that we move back to Hollywood as we are making no progress here. I wonder now whether the picture will ever be started, let alone finished.

JANUARY 14, 1961

A new bombshell—Skouras is considering another producer and director!

Charles Feldman, my agent, phoned at 11 A.M. to impress on me that everything is my fault! I shouldn't listen to Liz, Skouras, Mamoulian, or anybody. I should shoot the script I have, then get retakes later.

He said I am letting Liz run the show, and I must stop that at once. He told me that Skouras wants to change the producer and director on the film and is talking with Mark Robson, who doubles in brass.

JANUARY 16, 1961

Disastrous meeting with Rogell, Mamoulian, and myself.

Mamoulian arrived at Rogell's office late—it was his wife Azadia's birthday and he had been at lunch with her. When Rogell criticized him for being late the hostility which had been below the surface burst to the top.

Rogell blamed Mamoulian for the delays; Mamoulian in turn blamed the executives. I tried to take some of the blame to pacify things but the meeting ended with Mamoulian furious and sulking, and Rogell determined to start shooting, hot or cold, on Thursday—Liz willing.

Mamoulian agreed without enthusiasm.

JANUARY 17, 1961

Met with Liz, Eddie, and Mamoulian about the script. Liz said it was terrible. Mamoulian, who had approved the script, ended up by siding with her and letting me take the blame for it.

JANUARY 18, 1961

Mamoulian resigns.

Saw Rouben this morning in Rogell's office. The meeting ended with Rouben and me having our first row. It started when I accused him of not standing up for the script the night before. He informed me he had cabled Skouras that he wants to resign.

I told him that he had made a mistake. If he had told me what he was going to do I never would have let him do it. I know the climate—they are considering his removal anyway and are talking to other directors.

"I didn't tell you because I knew you would have tried to stop me," Rouben said angrily. "I had made up my mind."

I think he is maneuvering for complete autonomy, but I believe he made a bad tactical error.

JANUARY 19, 1961

Skouras accepted Mamoulian's resignation. No shooting. Mamoulian's resignation and negotiations with Joe Mankiewicz are in the papers already. They are hinting that the next to resign will be Liz.

JANUARY 20, 1961

Rouben held a press conference. Barry Norman of the *Daily Mail* gave the following account of it:

WHY I QUIT "CLEO"
I had a dream, says Director.

Mr. Rouben Mamoulian chewed the end off a 6-inch cigar last night and tried to explain why he had resigned as director of the £3,000,000 film, CLEOPATRA.

"It cannot be made the way I want it," he said at his flat in Eaton Square, S.W.

"When I began fifteen months ago I had a dream, an artistic conception of the way the film should be. Now a number of things have made me realize the dream cannot become reality."

What dashed his dreams? It was not Elizabeth Taylor. It was not Mr. Spyros Skouras, head of 20th Century-Fox.

So what was the reason? "Elements," said 62-year-old Mr. Mamoulian vaguely. "Dreams have to be translated into flesh and blood. All manner of things, internal and external, get in the way."

JANUARY 23, 1961

Liz called. Wanted to know if she's in or out of the picture. Am I in or out?

Mamoulian is looking for support from Liz, who likes to stand up for the underdog, but it is too late. Skouras knows she will quiet down if he brings in Mankiewicz, whom she trusts and believes in.

Meanwhile, I am at my wit's end. There is still the problem of the script, and our overhead piles up—around $45,000 a day. We have only about ten minutes of film, some of it beautiful but none of it with Liz. And Liz refuses to do anything until the director hassle is settled.

JANUARY 25, 1961

Mankiewicz is hired as writer-director. Skouras wants JLM to run the show. There is already conflict between Skouras and JLM over JLM's *insistence* that I continue to be producer of *Cleopatra*.

Where Rouben is slow moving and a chain cigar-smoker, Joe is mercurial and a pipe-smoker. JLM is intelligent with a wonderful sense of humor. Rouben is also intelligent, but has less sense of humor. The main difference between these two men is their ability to adapt to situations. Mamoulian is unbending as is JLM, but JLM is much more adept in handling touchy matters.

FEBRUARY 1, 1961

Mankiewicz begins to take over.

He has arrived in London with an entirely new, modern, psychiatrically rooted concept of the film. It is one with which I can agree entirely and I believe it can lead to a great picture. Mark Antony lived always in the shadow of Caesar—Caesar's trusted lieutenant, Caesar's loyal friend, Caesar's right hand—but never a Caesar. JLM sees Antony as a bad replica of Caesar, following desperately in Caesar's footsteps, but rattling loosely in them on the battlefield, in the Senate and in Caesar's bed. He sees this inability to match Caesar as the cause of Antony's excessive drinking and eccentric behavior. Antony's conquest of Cleopatra is his only triumph over Caesar. Then he realizes he has not conquered but has been conquered—and this leads to his ultimate self-destruction.

JLM sees Cleopatra as one of the very first women to rule in a man's world—a woman who wanted it all and picked off the Number One and Number Two ranking men of that world in succession. Cleopatra is not a wide-eyed child in his concept. She is an artist of consummate femininity, a genius in the art of attracting men. His overall approach is through the story of the woman who nearly made it.

It is his plan to stay very close to history. The lives of our chief protagonists, as chronicled in Plutarch, Suetonius, Appian and other ancient sources, are crammed with dramatic event and structure. He is going to start the script with the battle of Pharsalia.

JLM comes in the midst of a crisis: the cast is in open rebellion against being required to play the original script, which conceives of Cleopatra as a virgin who could be deflowered only by a god. JLM says he cannot salvage anything from the original, and he plans to disregard it completely in favor of his own concept. In this case he has my enthusiastic OK, as well as Skouras'. But more will have to be discarded than the script and the 10½ minutes of film already shot—all the footage made during these disastrous ten weeks.

We must also pay off all the contract people like Peter Finch, who will receive $150,000 for the role he was not able to complete. We are recasting the entire production as well as replanning and rebuilding. And we need enough screenplay ready to enable us to start shooting here again as close to March 15 as possible.

A hurried call has gone out to writers to help organize and set down a story line which can be translated into a screenplay as quickly as possible.

FEBRUARY 5, 1961

Sidney Buchman and Lawrence Durrell, both of whom like the Mankiewicz concept, made themselves available for enough time to get us started at any rate. Durrell is to be paid $2,500 a week.

The modus operandi is to hold conferences plotting the story line section by section. Buchman and Durrell then prepare separate "story-step outlines" which Mankiewicz adapts and expands into his screenplay outline. The outline has to be detailed and as close to the eventual screenplay as possible because of the pressure of time.

FEBRUARY 9, 1961

Received a copy of budget report from Rogell. Total cost to date: $4,998,000. Estimated further cost to complete the picture: $4,866,000. The grand total is almost ten million dollars. What we have spent so far is, I am sure, wasted, and I doubt that we will ever finish the picture within this estimate.

February 14, 1961

The London *Evening Standard* reported that Fox is claiming almost twelve million dollars from the forty insurance companies and ninety syndicates of Lloyd's underwriters that insured us on the picture.

The paper also reported that Liz had won her libel suit against the *Daily Mail* for claiming *Cleopatra* had been held up because she was overweight.

February 16, 1961

I have seen the first pages of Mankiewicz's screenplay outline. Excellent!

JLM has begun dictating his screenplay outline to Elaine Schreyeck, who was his script girl on *Suddenly Last Summer*. She transcribes her shorthand notes in rough form. He corrects and edits them in longhand. Then the material is mimeographed. Luckily for us, JLM is including long passages of dialogue in his outline, but I have no idea when he is going to find time to write the actual screenplay.

Sidney Buchman has another assignment and can give us only a limited amount of time. Lawrence Durrell, who I consider a brilliant writer, seems a little baffled by the technique of screenwriting and dramaturgy, but he is whipping along on a shooting script based on the early pages of the JLM outline.

February 19, 1961

Visited Eddie at the London Clinic. While he and Liz were on holiday in Zurich he had an attack of appendicitis. In the rush of coming back for his operation here Liz caught Asian flu.

February 27, 1961

JLM told me about Liz's birthday. Liz was in bed at the Dorchester, still suffering from Asian flu, but she had a party for the children. JLM, who dropped in to see her, said she put on a brave show for the children though she seemed ill.

MARCH 1, 1961

At last everything is going along beautifully. The plan is to start shooting in London April 4, then to Egypt for the exteriors.

MARCH 3, 1961

9:30 A.M. JLM called me about Liz. He is beginning to worry. He has talked with Dr. Goldman, who said she is "quite ill."

MARCH 4, 1961

Eddie called this morning, distraught over Liz, who he said is seriously ill. She is being attended by eleven doctors, including the Queen's physician. She has staphylococcus pneumonia.

Eddie called back to ask if I could possibly find a portable toilet! I rushed to Harrod's, got one, and hurried back to their hotel. There I learned that Lord Evans had been able to supply one—reportedly the same one used by her Majesty the Queen on tours to the more primitive corners of the Empire.

At the hotel I heard that doctors have given Liz only one hour to live unless surgery is performed to open her windpipe and ease congestion. Eddie called Hollywood for Dr. Kennamer.

In the evening Liz was rushed in an ambulance with Eddie by her side from the Dorchester to the London Clinic. A tracheotomy was performed. I hurried to the clinic and fought my way through the crowds of press people but was unable to see Eddie. A reporter told me Liz was in an automatic respirator, something like an iron lung, to make breathing easier.

MARCH 5, 1961

A sleepless night with the telephone. My own doctor came to my home at 9 A.M. He gave me a sedative because he doesn't think

Liz in her condition has a chance to survive the operation and he wants me prepared for the worst.

The excitement and tension is incredible. The hospital issues health bulletins every fifteen minutes, so I am staying near my radio.

March 6, 1961

There was a news report today in America that Liz had died. Skouras called: "My God, how did it happen?" He sounded beside himself. I told him it was not true and the news report had been denied.

We are all very frightened and, it appears, so is the world. The streets around the hospital are crowded with reporters and cameramen checking everybody going in and out of the hospital. People crying; flowers and gifts and cures are coming in from all over the world.

JLM was at the hospital last night from 2 to 6 A.M., when the situation was critical. He had been sent for, as he is very close to Liz and Eddie. Sid Rogell called Skouras from my house to give him a personal report that she was improving.

I spoke to Eddie in the afternoon, who said the news was a little better—thank heavens. I went to the hospital but was unable to see Liz. Dr. Goldman said she has a tube in her windpipe to help her breathe. It may leave a scar about an inch long, he said, but it can be covered by plastic surgery later.

The picture, of course, has been postponed for the present.

March 6, 1961

Still can't get into the hospital without being photographed and interviewed, so I found a back way. Eddie was in an awful state. Dr. Goldman told me Liz is making progress and is much better. She is being fed intravenously and receiving blood transfusions.

JLM said she wrote a note asking to see her mother. Eddie is the only other person who has seen her.

March 7, 1961

News about Liz is a little better. I went to the clinic with Sid but was unable to see Liz. Her parents arrived, which is good.

March 9, 1961

Liz nearly out of danger. Eddie fine.

The messages to Liz from all over the world are unbelievable. The mail is stored in huge laundry baskets. Most of it is touching. For instance, "Six thousand of us are praying for you at the Boeing plant. We know you'll pull through." Wire from a U.S. destroyer saying, "Hooray for you, Liz, don't give up." Calls from doctors and wires offering assistance, even from Russia. The clinic has never been in such chaos.

March 11, 1961

The tube is finally out of her throat and she is uncomfortable and irritable. She has trouble breathing and is in a lot of pain.

Liz's Rolls came by my house to pick up some soup my cook had especially prepared for her. The cook, a great fan of Liz's, has occasionally made spaghetti for her, which is always picked up in grand style by the Rolls-Royce.

March 12, 1961

Saw Liz at the hospital. She looks marvelous, sitting up in bed drinking champagne and is in great humor. Truman Capote was also there visiting.

Skouras called. He is arriving Tuesday and is still terribly worried about Liz. "Do anything she wants to make her happy, and healthy. That's all that counts—forget about the picture," he said on the phone. No doubt about it, in his typically expansive way he is deeply concerned about her.

March 13, 1961

Skouras is not coming to London but called and told Sid Rogell and JLM they are to go to New York without me for conferences about the future of the picture.

March 14, 1961

Dr. Goldman says Liz is eating her first solids and custards. It will be August or September before she can go back to work. This is the news we are waiting for.

Skouras okays pulling down $600,000 worth of sets in London and has given us a starting date in Italy in September.

March 24, 1961

Sid Rogell called to say Eddie is insistent we film the picture in Hollywood. Eddie said he is taking matters into his own hands, as he is responsible for Liz and must protect her. It's his duty not to expose her to any more bad climate and he wants her near her Hollywood doctors. He said Liz is now walking and in good humor.

March 24, 1961

Met JLM and our staff at Pinewood to decide what to do about the English sets, props, and costumes. JLM and I are going to Rome in a few days to look for locations, and, following the week of surveying in Rome, JLM and production members will go to Egypt and all the way up the Nile looking for locations.

March 29, 1961

Liz and Eddie flew home to Hollywood.

There was a riot at the clinic today when they left on their way to the airport. The door was almost torn off her Rolls-Royce and she had to be moved from one car to another. Airport authorities told me Queen Elizabeth never had such a send-off as Elizabeth Taylor—an interesting contrast to her arrival in England, when she had such a ghastly reception from the press.

The picture is still up in the air waiting for doctors to confirm our new starting date. The only thing definite now is our return to Hollywood for the time being. I must get rid of my house in London and take Shelley, my youngest daughter, out of school. I thought I would be here for the rest of my life and gave out stories of that nature to the press. But here goes.

By evening, I was able to call Liz and Eddie in California. They had a good trip and are rarin' to start *Cleopatra* again. They are going to buy a house in California and settle there. "It's the only place in the world for us," Eddie said.

APRIL 15, 1961

Talked with JLM. The writer situation is acute. We discussed the possibility of Lillian Hellman, to give it the woman's touch, or Paul Osborn. I think JLM should do it himself if it is at all possible.

APRIL 19, 1961

Called Liz in California to congratulate her on the Oscar she won last night, which was big news here in London in the papers and on radio and television.

She was elated. "My legs are still a little wobbly," she said. "I haven't walked much since we've been home."

She told me she was so weak that Eddie and Dr. Kennamer had to help her up on stage to receive her Oscar and she said she and Eddie are still searching for a home in the Beverly Hills area.

Next month they are going to go to Las Vegas where Eddie will play for four weeks. Eddie got on the phone to quip: "I may work Liz into the act now that she's won an Oscar."

Cleopatra is tentatively set to start again in Hollywood this summer with locations in Rome and Egypt. Liz said she was ready and eager but still doesn't have permission to work yet from Dr. Kennamer. I made a date to meet with her in Hollywood sometime next week.

April 24, 1961

Leaving today for Hollywood—the fiasco in London is ended. We didn't make the film. We didn't even settle the hairdressers' strike. But Liz is still alive, and determined to make this the greatest picture ever made. The question is: when, where and how?

BOOK III

INTERMISSION IN HOLLYWOOD

[1961]

— HOLLYWOOD —

APRIL 25, 1961

The attitude here toward *Cleopatra* has changed. Bob Goldstein left London to take charge of the studio following Buddy Adler's death. Now he is behind the eight-ball himself; current product had not been successful, so he is mighty interested in having one good and big picture to the studio's credit.

Goldstein wants us to succeed, but he is in the middle of a gigantic tug of war between a minority group of shareholders and bankers and Skouras. The minority group, composed of John Loeb, of Loeb-Rhoades, one of the leading investment houses on Wall Street, lawyer Milton Gould, and investment broker Peter G. Treves, are attempting to force a change in management. They want to oust Goldstein and Skouras and elevate Peter Levathes, who is supposed to have done wonders for Fox in the field of television, to be in charge of the studio's film operation. Later they want him to not only head the studio but eventually become president of the corporation. This power struggle occupies the attention of almost every executive at the studio. Power politics is the order of the day, not picture making.

I was shocked, when I returned, to see the physical change on the lot. More than half of the studio back lot has been sold for a gigantic housing development, and construction crews are already at work on what will soon be Century City.

Also, most of the sound stages are busy with TV series. Only one or two motion pictures being filmed, and it looks as if the studio has decided its future lies in television.

Happily, however, the studio also seems convinced that the only films successful at the box office are blockbusters. Despite our Dunkirk in London they realize *Cleopatra* has the look and smell of bigness and potential success.

APRIL 25, 1961

Saw Liz at her bungalow at the Beverly Hills Hotel. I bought her a gift—a carved emerald of Cleopatra which came from Czar Nicholas' collection. Liz adores to have things given to her. She's like a child with gifts.

APRIL 26, 1961

JLM is finishing the treatment for his version of *Cleopatra*, and it's excellent. Bob Goldstein continues to be co-operative and pleasant with us.

APRIL 29, 1961

We have accomplished three things of importance in our first few days at the studio: writer Randall MacDougall was hired to do a new script from JLM's screenplay outline, for $75,000; Irene Sharaff agreed to design Elizabeth's costumes; Leon Shamroy was signed as cameraman.

MacDougall is a hard, fast worker and excellent researcher. He used to write documentaries for the BBC, and his work has a crisp, see-it-now flavor, but his scenes and dialogue are not in JLM's class and I suspect JLM will write his own script eventually.

I first approached Miss Sharaff, who is one of the top Broadway designers, to do costumes for *Cleopatra* in 1958. Irene, who is tall, sharp-eyed and candid, brushed it off with, "It wouldn't be possible to do *Cleopatra* without making it look like a production of *Aida*." Now, however, she admitted that some of the excitement of our concept of the picture had reached her and agreed to design Elizabeth's costumes.

Shamroy, invariably called Shammy, is a top cameraman, three-time Oscar winner and also one of the most colorful characters in Hollywood. A growling, cigar-smoking cynic, he has a wonderful sense of humor and grouses loudest when a picture is going well. When there are problems, he is happy—then he is in familiar territory.

Shammy is not only a trusted friend, but his personal insight is as keen as his camera's. For me, as well as for many other Hollywood producers, directors, and stars, he often serves as a kind of lay analyst. Also he is one of the best cameramen in the business. He was under contract to me in the Thirties and we made many fine pictures together, including *Private Worlds*.

April 30, 1961

The order of the day is: Make *Cleopatra* in Italy and Egypt during the months of September and October and shoot all interiors in Los Angeles in the winter on our wonderful, big, well-equipped stages.

We start making plans for that schedule—but carefully now—because we know that it was not the schedule yesterday and it probably will not be the schedule tomorrow. Every time we are given a starting date and a location date someone has to begin making commitments for space; someone else takes a trip to the area to find locations; cast and crew are hired and commitments made. And each change or cancellation costs money.

But Fox has had a long period without a hit. Skouras has a large, experienced, world-wide distribution organization which is keyed to handle lots of important product and isn't getting what it needs. The Old Boy is in a panic. He hopes and prays that *Cleopatra* will do for Fox what *Ben-Hur* did for MGM.

May 1, 1961

Skouras had promised the Board of Directors in New York a June start for *Cleopatra* and is raising hell over JLM's news that we won't have the script in time. A June start is completely out of the question.

MAY 2, 1961

Dr. Rex Kennamer, Elizabeth's close friend and Beverly Hills doctor, has given us the official go-ahead for her on filming locations in Italy in September. "Liz is in excellent health," he said.

MAY 5, 1961

Letter to Spyros Skouras:

Dear Spyros:

We feel that the meetings with you here during Monday, Tuesday, and Wednesday were most constructive and the decisions arrived at after the meeting with Dr. Rex Kennamer were completely sound and will enable us to make the picture the company wants under intelligent and correct organization. We are reviewing herewith the questions we were faced with and our answers:

Question 1. Why can't the film be started until September?

For many reasons, involving not only the size and scope of the picture itself, but also the health of Miss Taylor and the certainty we must have that she can successfully sustain the most grueling role of her entire career. We have taken advantage of the enforced layoff to improve the concept of the story we want to tell. The fact that we had to leave England necessitated tearing down all the sets. These must be redesigned and reconstructed here and abroad. Many of the costumes have yet to be designed and made. The very labor of crating and shipping the salvaged props from England would take almost three months.

As far as Miss Taylor is concerned she is still not fully

recovered from her illness, in the sense that her leg still bothers her. She has never looked more beautiful nor has she ever been more enthusiastic about the project. The scar on her neck will have to be removed by plastic surgery. Dr. Kennamer has informed us that this cannot be done until the early part of July. This means that she will not be available for testing wardrobe and make-up until the latter part of July.

Question 2. Isn't it true that if Elizabeth Taylor had not gotten sick you would have started the picture in England in April?

Of course this is true. We would have done the best we could. We would have attempted to rewrite the script as we made the picture, utilizing the sets that were already constructed. We would have been at the mercy of the uncertain English weather and there was no reason to suppose that our progress would not have been at least as expensive and the making of the picture as cumbersome as it was during the few weeks in which production had started previously.

The production of *Cleopatra* under those circumstances would have been hazardous and unsatisfactory. As it is, we are now able to undertake this great project properly prepared and under the best possible circumstances.

Question 3. Why are you shooting the locations first?

Because from every possible point of view it would be foolhardy to do anything else.

Dr. Kennamer has assured us that there is every reason to believe that Elizabeth's health will be at its best when we resume production. He has expressed his opinion that she is no more likely to become ill in Italy or Egypt than in California.

September, from the point of view of climate, is the finest month of the year in Italy.

Likewise, climatically speaking, October is Egypt's finest month. Location work with Miss Taylor is essential in both places.

It is our plan to finish her in Italy as soon as possible, then to finish her in Egypt as soon as possible—and then to return her to Hollywood for a rest, while the remainder of the cast finishes its foreign locations.

This means that during the winter months, Miss Taylor would be getting the advantage of shooting the interiors in California instead of being subjected to the risks of intemperate climates elsewhere.

As far as the film itself is concerned—it is difficult to think of any major production involving locations in which the locations have *not* been shot first. The reasons for this are obvious. Once the outdoor shooting is done, the indoor shooting can be adapted to match it. The reverse is difficult and costly. The outdoor scenes usually involve many actors who can finish their parts rather quickly after their scenes are shot. To shoot the interiors first would require carrying them on salary for many months. Next, the fact that a company knows it has its most arduous work behind it is a tremendous asset both in the morale and speed of shooting the interiors. Also, if extra scenes are required they can be picked up before the bad weather commences.

Question 4. Cleopatra will undoubtedly be the most ambitious and expensive project ever undertaken by 20th Century-Fox. Is it worth it?

No attraction in the history of show business has ever had the "want-to-see" publicity and demand from the public that *Cleopatra* with Elizabeth Taylor has had. The world-wide interest is considered unheard of in public "penetration" in every country where pictures are seen.

Consequently, the goal to achieve is not a compromise production or a film of expedience, but an original, exciting, romantic historical film that will enthrall the audience and achieve a record international gross. The reason that we feel this can be done is:

1. We are telling the amazing story of the most remarkable woman of all times, showing her entire life from the age of 19 to her dramatic death at 39 years of age. Covering for the first time in the theater the contrasting lives of Caesar and Antony and the enmity of Octavian. All of this against the greatest panorama of world conquest. The spectacular sequences, such as Cleopatra's entrance into Rome . . . the battle of Actium, and the orgies in Alexandria, will not be the stereotyped spectacles of the usual "big" pictures, but overall dramatic concepts never before on the screen. This picture, as now conceived, is one that every man, woman, and child should want to see. But in order to achieve this in an organized way, the logistics of this enterprise must be carefully organized and prepared in the next three months.

2. Yesterday we spent two hours with the production office in setting up all safeguards for the operation. A clear understanding of the objectives in all departments was agreed upon.

3. The script must be taut, gripping, exciting, and intelligent to satisfy the whole world market.

4. The cast must be superlative from an acting standpoint. Cleopatra could not be improved upon and Caesar and Antony must be the finest and strongest actors available, as well as all of the remaining cast.

5. The production must not look like a studio production. The beauty of Italy and Egypt will give this Todd-AO production a scope and authenticity that will lift the whole film to unique proportions.

6. The costumes, in the hands of the creative designers, will give a stamp of reality and style that will not have been seen before.

7. All the technical work is now being planned to be executed by Hollywood technicians, who are the best in the world.

8. The program is as follows:

During active preparation at the studio, Joseph Mankiewicz and staff will go to Italy and Egypt in two weeks to settle all problems regarding the locations so preparation can go forward. After two weeks, he will return to the studio to continue preparation. By the end of July, start tests with Elizabeth Taylor. In September, the film will commence in Italy with Elizabeth Taylor's scenes, then to Egypt for Elizabeth Taylor's scenes. As soon as her Italian and Egyptian work is finished, she will return to Hollywood to rest while Mankiewicz finishes his work in Italy and Egypt. Shooting will then commence in Hollywood on the interiors, probably by the end of October or first of November, and the company will remain here until completion.

We assure you we realize fully our responsibilities in being given the largest and most expensive production ever attempted by 20th Century-Fox and we will stop at nothing to give an attraction that will get you the largest profit and the most acclaim.

Kindest regards,
Walter

May 12, 1961

JLM cabled Skouras saying he was deeply disturbed and disheartened by his refusal to approve Richard Burton as Mark Antony. JLM pointed out that we do not have to face the problem of box-office attraction (because of Elizabeth) so it does not matter whether Burton is not considered a box-office star.

JLM pointed out Burton's "physical attractiveness and impressive personality" and described him as a "magnificent and experienced actor with the technical resources and dramatic power I can draw upon not only to sustain but to realize completely that all important second half" of the picture.

He closed the wire by noting that the production staff and studio administration are in complete agreement that Burton should play Mark Antony and said there is a very good chance we would lose him unless Skouras withdrew his objection quickly.

May 13, 1961

Eddie's "surprise party" for Liz.

The party was given at Au Petit John in Beverly Hills and everyone in town seemed to be there. I noticed Kurt Frings in a heated, obviously confidential discussion with Jack Warner, which I understand went on until 4 A.M.

May 14, 1961

Gary Cooper died. Services tomorrow. Another good friend gone. I was at Paramount when he was first signed and we have been friends ever since.

May 18, 1961

JLM suggested that the studio assign a new production number to this version of *Cleopatra* and the old budget not be included with the new. A very good move on his part—to keep the English cost from being added to our budget. Our new number is "JO4."

May 19, 1961

JLM and I have finally convinced Skouras that Burton is the right man to play Mark Antony.

Now it's a question of negotiations, which will probably be complicated, as he is a hit on Broadway in *Camelot*. JLM to leave tomorrow for Rome and Cairo to scout locations, as it is definite we will do some location work in these places. I remain in Hollywood to organize production, get Elizabeth's wardrobe started, and the script finished.

MAY 21, 1961

Called Liz in Las Vegas.

The papers report she is there every night for Eddie's show, arriving at the room where he is entertaining just before he goes on. He sings his last song, *That Face*, directly to her. The audience loves it. So does Liz.

I sent some of Irene's costumes to Liz for fittings but her back is still bothering her. We will send the fitters to Vegas.

JUNE 2, 1961

Talked with Eddie Fisher in Las Vegas.

Liz has laryngitis. Eddie told me Frings and Warner were working out a big deal for him and Liz. "It's the biggest deal ever made, and if Fox doesn't handle the rest of *Cleopatra* properly we won't finish it."

I told Pete Levathes, who is now in charge of the studio, about the Warner deal with Liz and Eddie. He said there is nothing to it. Fox is about to sign Liz to a four-picture deal to follow *Cleopatra*.

JUNE 5, 1961

Talked to Jerry Wald about the Wall Street bankers who seem to be taking over the studio.

All the producers on the lot are frustrated. Wald, George Stevens, David O. Selznick have each run studios but they can't get anybody in authority here to discuss their picture problems. They spend hours of each week being interviewed by bankers. In the big struggle for power Skouras is working skillfully to win over the minority stockholders group.

JUNE 7, 1961
Excerpts from a letter to JLM:

Dear Joe:

I am sorry that I missed your call from Rome; however, the wire to Merman to have me stand by didn't arrive until the day after you spoke. And I did wait as long as I could after I received the wire from Johnny, but I had a very serious dental appointment and I would have much rather talked to you than to have been in the dentist chair.

We have all missed you, but I will try to get you up to date on what has been happening, roughly, as far as I know . . .

Randy has been most industrious about turning out copy. I have taken him off for two days to complete the treatment, so that, in the event that you feel that we should show it to Burton, we would have something to show him, as he has been screaming for a treatment, or script, or something.

I have spoken to Elizabeth several times, and Eddie, and they have apparently changed their plans again and are not going to Europe immediately, as Eddie is going to open at the Ambassador Hotel on July 25th. They sent their love to you and wanted to know where you were and where they can get in touch with you. She is naturally very excited about Burton. I explained to her that we had a very good chance of getting him, but that we hadn't closed as yet . . .

John Loeb's associate, Woodfin, is here. Also Gould, who is the head of the new committee, and Treves, whom Gould represents. There are all sorts of rumors flying, and every kind of strange scheme being evolved. The last I heard was that Skouras was going to be moved out here to help Bob Goldstein run the studio, because Skouras was so efficient in production. This was the bankers' latest finding. My own feeling is that Skouras will outwit the whole crowd because I saw the bankers going home last night with books under their arms, and they are now discussing scripts, and Ray Stark gave a party for them and introduced them to a lot of starlets.

Skouras was negotiating, as you know, with Liz for four pictures, but kept it very quiet. So quiet that he overplayed his hand and Liz and Eddie are supposed to be making a deal with Warner Brothers for four pictures. However, it is not an exclusive deal and I have talked to Liz and Eddie about the situation and they are in the position that, if we want her for *Justine*, I am sure that she will be available.

I have been looking at a lot of Negro actors and actresses, hoping to find a good Charmion and a good Apollodorus. So far, I have seen certain possibilities and I am going to try and see some in New York. I am sure that we will find what we want. I have seen some very striking types that I think will be very useful in other parts of the picture and especially in the Procession into Rome.

I am turning them over to Hermes Pan, whom I have been talking to, and I have had Hermes look at the designs for the procession as Novarese sees it. Hermes has some very fine ideas which I am pretty sure are going to please you tremendously.

Incidentally, I ran into an Egyptologist the other day who came up with the idea that it was a great mistake to call it "Cleopatra's Barge," because it should have been known as "The Royal Galley." Personally, I don't know whether a galley is better than a barge, but maybe it is.

I have told Rosemary to make a one-line continuity of the treatment from beginning to end, so that you can have that to compare to the script and it might be very useful when we get to editing and cutting.

Needless to say, the studio is in the height of confusion, but, so far, nobody seems to be worrying too much . . .

With every good wish—as always,
Walter F. Wanger

P.S. Zeus [Skouras], of course, is here. I have seen him twice today . . . once on the Taylor deal, which I am trying to get back on the track for Fox . . . and, secondly, on Burton. The price of 250 has been approved, but we are asking for thirty weeks. I doubt if we will get it, but I think that it is a fair request. I will probably be seeing him while I am in New York.

— NEW YORK —

JUNE 8, 1961

Went to see *Camelot* and Richard Burton. I thought him dynamic and forceful—a perfect Mark Antony, as JLM conceives him.

After the show I visited Burton in his dressing room. He was surrounded by fans, autograph seekers, and well-wishers. He was very affable. A young lady named Pat remained behind after the others had left, and Burton asked if she could join us at "21." Burton entered the restaurant like a football hero at a college prom with the prettiest cheerleader at school on his arm. He exuded confidence, personality, and sex appeal.

He said he was excited about working with JLM, whom he knew well and had great respect for. When I pointed out that we were still only in the negotiation stage for him he said, "Don't worry. I want to do this. We will work out a deal." I hope so.

— HOLLYWOOD —

JUNE 12, 1961

JLM back from Rome enthusiastic about locations. He does not want to shoot in Egypt if he can help it.

Skouras in town. Going through the crowded lunchroom he said to me sadly, "Look at all this talent here, and our pictures turn out bad." He should know the answer: there's no one at the head of the studio, no one to run things, who understands production problems of modern picture making.

During these weeks there have been many meetings with the executives, including Skouras who seemed to commute from New York. At meeting after meeting he calls JLM and by-passes me. But Joe calls me, says, "I think you ought to be at the meetings," and insists that I go in with him.

I was in a delicate position with Joe. I knew that the studio was high on him and had given him complete authority, but I felt that since I am producer and it is my company's project it is my duty and obligation to get the script written the way we planned it. Like most artists JLM is sensitive to criticism or being pushed, so he had to be handled with great tact and diplomacy.

Brought Liz together with Irene Sharaff for the first time. An important meeting because I want them to like each other. Thank heavens, it came off well.

JUNE 13, 1961

Levathes raised the roof about Burton's contract, which is still being negotiated. He wants to reduce it to $200,000 for thirty weeks.

Levathes asked me if I would take over Skouras' convention plans. As I understand the situation, Skouras is worried about the morale of the theater exhibitors and salesmen handling Fox films, which have not been too successful lately. He wants to have a convention and banquet here at the studio—on a *Cleopa-*

tra set—and has given orders to rush a set into production. His plan is to put on a big show for the exhibitors and salesmen to impress them with future product and create an atmosphere of progress.

I complained about the set being built on our budget and refused to handle the convention for the studio.

JUNE 26, 1961

The studio situation is a mess. Skouras and Levathes lost the four-picture deal they planned to make with Liz, and they are upset.

The studio is still overrun with Wall Street associates, asking all kinds of questions about picture making. As a result, Levathes has gone on an efficiency kick, but I think it's too late.

Liz and Eddie went to the Russian Ballet in Los Angeles and gave a party for the dancers later. The dancers, in turn, invited the Fishers to visit them in Russia. Liz and Eddie accepted the invitation and plan to go next month.

JUNE 30, 1961

We are to shoot all of *Cleopatra* in Italy!

Most of the stage space here is taken up with television, and what is left is needed for George Stevens' *Greatest Story Ever Told*, so it was suddenly decided to get us off the lot.

Called Liz to tell her the news, and she didn't seem too happy about it. She is worried about getting a good place to live in Rome. I told her we'd start looking for her. She was also very anxious to get Roddy McDowall in the picture. I said JLM and myself want Roddy too, and we are working on it. Eddie was not enthusiastic about going to Italy. He has many deals here and I don't think he is anxious to go away, because he is worried about Liz being so far away from her doctors.

News of the sudden change in plan was relayed instantly to Johnny Johnston and John DeCuir who were contacted at New

York's Idlewild Airport where they were enroute to Italy to set up locations only.

July 7, 1961

JLM busy helping Liz write a speech she is going to deliver at a fund-raising banquet for Cedars of Lebanon Hospital.

July 9, 1961

Elizabeth's speech, about how it feels to be near death, was an enormous success. It was so dramatic and vivid that the audience pledged almost seven million dollars.

July 11, 1961

My birthday! Liz and Eddie to Moscow.

July 18, 1961

Liz and Eddie back from Moscow and talking about doing a picture in Russia. They are anxious to get started on *Cleopatra*. Liz in fine health.

July 25, 1961

Still in a muddle about Burton.

Ordinarily I would close a deal like this myself, but at Fox the signing of an important actor becomes a major operation involving the casting department here and in New York, legal departments on both coasts, New York executives, etc. The studio has a lot of people who have to be kept busy.

July 26, 1961

Went to Western Costume to see Irene Sharaff's costumes for Liz. They are marvelous—Irene really is a genius and wonderful to work with.

Liz has postponed her date for fittings. I suspect she gained weight on the Russian trip, which means she's on a crash diet again. She likes clothes to fit skin tight. One or two pounds can make a difference, and Liz is always concerned about looking her best, naturally.

JULY 27, 1961

Excerpts from a letter to JLM in Rome:

> . . . We are still counting on a starting date of September 18th. If this is to be changed, please advise us as soon as possible, as it will affect actors' starting dates. I am very anxious to know what date you want Liz and if there is any news on villas. I haven't heard a thing from Rosemary or Johnny on either matter.
>
> Eddie's opening was not nearly as effective as Vegas because the room was so large and the whole rat pack was there and they finally got up on the stage and it became a real Hollywood evening, if you know what I mean.
>
> With love to all.
> As always,
> Walter F. Wanger

JULY 29, 1961

JLM sent a telegram to Owen McLean, casting director at 20th Century-Fox, complaining that with the starting date of the picture only seven weeks away only six of approximately forty-six principal roles had been cast.

AUGUST 1, 1961

Irene Sharaff upset because Liz has not yet come in for fittings or given a date when she will come. Irene is not used to working this way. I explained that Liz would come when she felt she was in shape.

JLM now in Rome without a sufficient production staff. He's

trying to do everything himself, which is ridiculous. It's unfair to bother him with all these extraneous problems and expect him to turn out a great script which has to satisfy three of the most important artists in the world.

AUGUST 2, 1961

The villa for Liz and Eddie in Rome is becoming a problem.

In this picture the producer also fills in as janitor and general handy man. At 2 A.M. I finally got through to a Princess in Rome who is in the real-estate business. She said she would look for something for the Fishers.

AUGUST 4, 1961

Eddie insists that Elizabeth's personal physician, Dr. Rex Kennamer, go to Rome with them—at company expense. Dr. Kennamer's fee is $25,000 plus expenses for the six weeks he will be in Rome.

AUGUST 4, 1961

Excerpts from a letter to JLM:

> Dear Joseph,
>
> I thought that your interview on arrival in Rome was just fabulous. I sent the copy I got from Ascarelli over to Elizabeth. Incidentally, I'm working now trying to organize a really proper, world-wide organization to handle the publicity and exploitation of the picture. Einfeld is reluctant to spend any money and that, confidentially, is because of the pressures on him by the new members of the board who are trying to eliminate him; and Harry Brand at this end doesn't want to work with Einfeld if he can help it. So, between the two, I'll try to get the new board to meet with Pete Levathes

to set up something that is commensurate with the type of effort that you are making.

. . . Peter Levathes has been pressing me for the script, which I have refused to give him, and he is also very money-conscious now due to the presence here of the board members, including John Loeb. They all have the orthodox, Wall Street point of view of that operation. However, I have naturally refused to let him have the script, and told him that they'd just better be patient and come through with the money if they want a great picture. I found out the budget they hope for is six million on the first version, eight million for this version. The intrigue and conversation are very brutal and wild . . .

AUGUST 9, 1961

Levathes says Kennamer's fee is outrageous and refuses to okay it.

Irene unhappy because Liz wanted her to come to her bungalow for fittings because her arm hurts from shots. Irene refused. Liz out tonight at Kirk Douglas' party, and, presumably, is better and ready to work tomorrow.

AUGUST 10, 1961

Eddie's birthday.

Liz came to the studio for fittings and was very pleasant and slim. Liz and Irene getting on famously.

AUGUST 13, 1961

Talked with JLM in Rome, who said we are getting off to a bad start.

England all over again: we do not have a script, the sets aren't ready, costumes aren't ready. The props are not ready either and we need more than a million dollars' worth. We are being forced to begin shooting next month so Skouras can keep the Board of Directors quiet and because of the starting date on Liz's contract.

August 16, 1961

Unable to make a deal with Trevor Howard as Caesar. I called JLM in Rome and recommended Rex Harrison, who, I think, will be better in the long run. JLM agrees so we are going after him.

August 22, 1961

Now the villa for Eddie and Liz has become a crisis. Eddie says they won't go to Rome unless they have the right place to live. He suggests we send Bob Abrams, a friend and associate of his, to Rome to look. We have agreed to do this—at company expense.

August 25, 1961

Enroute to Rome stopped in New York to see Skouras. He was livid over an interview with Elizabeth in a recent *Look* magazine in which she said, "It will be fun to be the first Jewish Queen of Egypt." The statement was annoying to the Egyptian government, which had promised us co-operation.

— ROME —

August 27, 1961

Arrived here embarrassed and discouraged.

Embarrassed because of a story in the *Rome Daily American* which sounded as though JLM was doing nothing until I arrived. We were promised a retraction Tuesday.

Discouraged because once again we were under the gun to start the film. JLM had advised Skouras it would be cheaper to keep Liz on salary while we took time to prepare, but the attitude as always was, "For God's sake, get something on film."

Talking to the people at Fox is like a Kafka play in which you call a number, and no one's at the other end of the phone. You try to reason but discover no one is listening. Again we were about to attempt to film in opposition to every basic tenet of the professional film maker. We had no sets, no script, and no proper administrative organization. Although Johnny Johnston is in charge of production, the problems were way too big for one man. He is sick as well. When MGM made *Ben-Hur* in Rome they had three powerful production men and a staff working for over a year in advance and still had plenty of problems.

AUGUST 28, 1961

John DeCuir is complaining about the lack of stage space.

DeCuir, a good-looking, dedicated young man who is an ardent Catholic and goes to church every morning, is working non-stop on the design of sets. He will take all the abuse in the world without listening to anyone; he just goes on building and building. He has a great imagination combined with a terrible habit of elevating everything on platforms, which makes his sets difficult to light and photograph.

When I arrived here, he said we had an awful space problem: there was no room for the throne room on any of the stages at Cinecitta. He suggested we take over the DePaulis Studio, the biggest in Europe. It is, however, three quarters of an hour from Rome and from Cinecitta; it has no heating, no lights and no air-conditioning. When I pointed this out to DeCuir he smiled dreamily and said, "But there is space."

I told him I wouldn't hear of using another studio. If we did, Liz would have to make up here, then drive to the other studio. It was just too much trouble for all concerned. DeCuir went away unhappily, muttering that there wasn't room enough here for his throne room but he'd try to cram it someplace.

Talked with a real-estate man about a villa for the Fishers. Abrams is looking constantly but is having trouble finding the right place—they want a lot of space and a lot of bathrooms. Not everyone with a palazzo is anxious to rent to the Fishers, because they have too many animals and too many children.

AUGUST 28, 1961

JLM gave the crew of 100 technicians from Hollywood and England a pep talk about relations with Italian workers. He said: "Please bear in mind that if it is difficult to communicate with the Italians, the reason is that *you* do not speak *their* language. *Not* that they do not speak yours . . ." Good to remember any place and any time.

SEPTEMBER 1, 1961

Liz and Eddie arrived in Rome today with Dr. Kennamer, whose fee was finally approved.

We had to set squadrons of police to protect Liz from the *paparazzi*—Rome's jackal-like photographers. Photos of Liz are worth a small fortune and the photographers here are the most aggressive and obnoxious in the world.

The Fishers and the doctor went off immediately for a cruise on Sam Spiegel's yacht.

SEPTEMBER 2, 1961

Skouras arrived today looking tired.

For the first time I had the feeling that the operating committee of bankers who had been investigating the studio had gotten to him. They canceled the Stevens picture, *The Greatest Story Ever Told*, without asking for Skouras' opinion or okay. That picture was a dream of his and he was heartbroken. Apparently the bankers are getting very tough with him. I think he came to Rome to get away from them.

Before we got to Rome a deal had been made with Prince

Borghese to rent his private beach at Anzio for $150,000. After we started to build the Alexandria set there we found the beach was the one where the Allied troops landed. It was still mined!

I went to the beach, where an army of workers was clearing ground. One bulldozer struck an unexploded shell. We had to call in demolition experts to lug live ammunition away. More delays—and danger. All we need is to have a shell blow up and hurt some of our people!

In addition, I learned that the beach is next door to the NATO firing range, which means we will have to arrange our schedule so we are not working when the big guns are blasting. We will have to get NATO permission to be allowed on our own set!

September 5, 1961

Abrams called from Naples to say that Liz and Eddie had fallen in love with a 70-year-old Greek cook on the yacht. They want me to arrange to bring him to Rome.

September 6, 1961

The press clamor here in Rome is incredible. We are getting requests from all over the world from correspondents who want to interview Liz or see the sets being constructed.

Fathi Ibrahim, head of the Fox operation in Egypt, arrived today. Colorful and influential, Fathi speaks perfect English and handles himself like a character actor in a play. He is smooth, understanding, and able to get things done in a quiet way—but it must be his way. He is also very good on social contacts. His wife, Mary, is a charming woman, a real beauty, and the niece of the Emperor of Ethiopia.

At head of public relations is Giulio Ascarelli, an Italian-born American citizen, a real savvy guy who knows all the press in Rome, Paris, and London.

Tall, thin, and distinguished looking, Giulio is a worldly character who loves good things and a good life. Part of his future, however, is based on the income he expects to get from the Fox pension plan. He has been with the studio a long time and he intends to do the best job possible for us—without endangering his position. I fear he can be handled easily by Skouras.

SEPTEMBER 7, 1961

Finally got a chance to look over Cinecitta. The studio where we plan to work is very much like any Hollywood studio—for which I am partly responsible. When I was in Rome in 1936 I stayed with Dorothy de Frasso and her husband, the Count de Frasso at their Villa Madama, a fabulous palace with ceilings by Michelangelo, which was later used by Goering during the war.

One day they arranged for me to meet Mussolini, who was then at the peak of his power. Il Duce told me he wanted to build a film studio in Rome and asked for my suggestions.

I told him he ought to send someone to America—which he did. A very bright and wealthy engineer, Senator Roncaroni, who owned a racing stable in Rome, came to visit me in Hollywood. I showed him around, arranged for him to get blueprints of the major studios, including Fox, and he returned to Rome and designed Cinecitta.

Although we are not the only company shooting at Cinecitta we have certainly brought a circus flavor to the lot and to Rome. In one area an army of Italian men is being drilled to fight mighty land battles. An hour away at Anzio, ships were being constructed for the naval engagement at Actium, and Cleo's royal barge was being fitted with purple sails just like the ones the real Cleopatra's barges had.

Our sails, however, were of modern nylon because silk or cotton sails fade in the sun.

On the Borghese hunting estate on the Anzio beachhead, ancient Alexandria was being rebuilt and in Rome, half a mile from the real Forum, we were constructing a movie Forum larger than the original, where Caesar will welcome Cleopatra.

Our dance director, Hermes Pan, has been rehearsing hundreds of dancing girls for months, preparing them for the big procession scene when Cleopatra enters Rome.

A Negro ballet is on one of the sound stages rehearsing; athletes are practicing pole vaulting and swordplay in the athletic field, with archers shooting nearby; the charioteers—mostly Hollywood stunt men who worked in *Ben-Hur*—are working out on one of the outdoor sets. Some people are in costume, some out of costume, since the wardrobe department can't keep up with our needs.

SEPTEMBER 9, 1961

Elizabeth's dressing room is not ready yet.

An entire building is being redesigned for her. Eddie is upset over his problems, so they have become mine now: a station wagon, a cook, the Greek chef, and an upcoming photographic interview with *Life*.

With the exception of the cast, everyone associated with the film now wears a numbered, silver-dollar-sized badge. They come in three colors: blue for production, yellow for construction, and red for visitors. My badge is Number 11.

SEPTEMBER 11, 1961

Negotiations finally concluded for Rex Harrison to play Caesar, at $10,000 a week plus expenses, a car and driver, and co-star billing.

Roddy McDowall, Hume Cronyn, and half a dozen others signed for co-starring and feature roles.

Actors are arriving from all over the world every day. Some of them are not met at the plane because of our transportation problems. And the housing department occasionally messes up on getting the right accommodations, which makes for more chaos.

September 12, 1961

The handmaidens and the slave girls are on strike!

They claim the costumes they wear in the movie are too skimpy. Thank heavens for Magli, the Italian production manager. He pointed to the line of Italian male workers ogling and cheering the girls in the picket line, and proved that the costumes they wore to picket in were skimpier by far than their movie costumes.

Liz on time for tests today. She couldn't be in better spirits or more co-operative.

But we are having problems with the costumes—I fear sabotage. Some of them were mysteriously ripped, seams torn, none of them perfect. Rogell has sent to the Coast for Courtney Haslem, the studio wardrobe chief, to come here and reorganize the costume situation. An excellent idea, since we have 20,000 costumes.

A problem with Rex's costumes. During the period we were negotiating for him, Rex was working in a play in London and going to fittings after work. Apparently he didn't pay much attention to the costumes. We are all unhappy about his wardrobe. We have asked Irene Sharaff to re-do his entire wardrobe. Another delay but well worth it.

September 13, 1961

Liz was on set before 10 A.M. and in high spirits.

Her dressing room suite is completed. When Liz saw it for the first time she said with some surprise, "Isn't this a bit much?"

Although she never asked for it, she ended up with an entire building converted for her use. It includes an office for Eddie, a salon, a special room for her wigs, a dressing room, and a makeup room with bath and shower.

September 14, 1961

Johnny Johnston has come up with a $14 million budget and a report that Skouras is "upset."

Skouras claims the budget shouldn't be more than eight million dollars. JLM, who is always forthright, has told Skouras that we already are committed to more than ten million, but apparently Skouras is keeping some of the facts from the Board of Directors. This means we are making the picture on two budgets: the unrealistic New York budget, and the actual costs.

SEPTEMBER 21, 1961

Skouras arrived. We spent a difficult day in budget meetings.

Skouras said that unless budget was under eight, the Board of Directors would cancel the production. JLM handed Skouras the phone and said, "Greatest favor you could do the board would be to call them at once and say this film will cost a great deal over ten. Shall I put the call through for you?"

Skouras turned white and put down the phone. "We have to cut the budget somehow," he said.

That ended the meeting with JLM.

Later in the afternoon Skouras called a big meeting in my office with different department heads. "The budget is cut to ten million dollars," he said with finality.

Ridiculous—we had spent at least ten million dollars by the time of his announcement.

SEPTEMBER 22, 1961

Skouras very flattering to me and pleased with JLM, which worries me. He must have something in mind.

Liz and Eddie finally found a villa. It is in a little park, about seven minutes from the studio and near one of the Middle East embassies. The Villa Papa is a magnificent place, more like a California ranch house than an Italian villa.

It stands in eight acres of parklike grounds with beautiful pools and huge trees. The villa itself, California ranch style, contains seven bedrooms, six bathrooms, a huge living room, another smaller salon, and a well-appointed dining room.

The villa—rented for $3,000 a month—is ideal for the Fishers because the children can have one section of the house, and Liz and Eddie the other. The animals—five dogs, including a St. Bernard, collie, three small terriers; and two Siamese cats—have the run of the place.

SEPTEMBER 23, 1961

L'Unitá, the Communist daily, headlines that "*Cleopatra* is an Italian Little Rock." They claim that our white and colored dancers have to take separate buses, eat separately, and use different dressing rooms. Somehow they put the blame on Liz.

We denied the story instantly, but the matter actually came up in the Italian Parliament. Meanwhile, a collective letter signed by over sixty members (both white and colored) of the dance groups, including such people as Leo Coleman and Claude Marchant, protested strongly against the false charges. The letter was sent to left-wing papers which, nevertheless, never made any retraction.

Now it's elephant and horse trouble.

The horses won't work with the elephants in the big procession. Magli, our Italian production manager, has a relative who owns a troupe of elephants which we hired. The elephants, however, won't do what they're supposed to do, and one of the beasts is, I am sure, mad. He started to pull up some stakes, which caused Cinecitta to tell us we had to get the elephants out. We are writing to England for more elephants.

The cameras haven't started to turn yet and we already have one lawsuit against us. Santi's company, Galatea Films, is suing us for "notable damages" of a million dollars for not fulfilling our agreement made with him in 1959. We are in the papers every day without any assistance from the entertainment editor. Something newsworthy always seems to be happening.

September 24, 1961

The first scene of the movie, to be shot tomorrow, is of Cleopatra going to the temple to pray to the goddess Isis. JLM and I visited the set today to look it over, and the statue of Isis looks comic rather than imposing. We have a crew working all night remodeling it.

JLM is writing in longhand every day, laboring over the script, trying to get it as near right as possible. We are waiting for the costumes to be completed and fitted. Of the sixty sets needed only one is ready.

Every day that we are not before the cameras costs us $67,000 in overhead. So, tomorrow—ready or not—we start the picture.

BOOK IV

CLEOPATRA AND CAESAR

[1961–1962]

September 25, 1961

Today, finally, after years of work and headaches, we shot the first scene of *Cleopatra*.

Since our starting date coincided with the 100th anniversary of Italian unification, Treves, who is an enthusiastic Italian-American as well as one of the minority leaders in the Fox fight, promoted a junket to Italy for eleven U. S. Congressmen. As a highlight of the junket he promised to bring them to Cinecitta with their wives.

I said they could come to the studio but not on the set. Liz was working in a revealing costume. I knew that like the rest of us she would be likely to have first-day nerves—we had been through so much for so long in getting the picture started.

Predictably, the band of Congressmen with wives showed up at the studio wanting photographs taken everywhere, most especially with Elizabeth. They were taken on a full tour, finally ending up at our Forum set across the street from the set where we were shooting. I went to the Forum and announced over the loudspeaker that because of the pressure of the first day of shooting Miss Taylor would not be available, but that we had a cocktail party planned for later.

Some of the Congressmen, however, got tired of waiting and angrily left the studio. When Elizabeth heard what happened, she invited the Congressmen and wives who remained to come to her dressing room where they had some drinks and pleasant conversation.

September 26, 1961

I learn that our eager publicity department had given out in advance "Press Release No. 2," which said, "On their tour of the Forum set, the group of Congressmen was accompanied by Elizabeth Taylor, who left her set for the specific purpose of greeting them." No wonder there was a misunderstanding as the papers reported today, with poor Liz catching the blame.

September 28, 1961

Elizabeth is truly Queen of Rome.

Shooting stopped at 5:30 today so Liz could go home to get dressed for an appearance tonight at the Sistine Theater. She is to be awarded the Maschera d'Argento (Silver Mask) for her performance in *Suddenly Last Summer*. A big honor, as the award is the Italian equivalent of an Oscar.

Liz was wearing a fabulous silver evening gown with a neckline that plunged to the waist. The mob went wild when they saw her enter the theater. When she went on stage, it took about forty uniformed and plain-clothes policemen to stop the paparazzi from rushing right up to the stage to take pictures of Liz. About sixty photographers eventually ran into the wings where they took turns standing on each other's shoulders to get pictures.

After the award ceremonies the photographers literally fought with the police to get pictures, while a mob of 2,000 or more screaming Italians overwhelmed Liz and Eddie.

Eddie pushed Liz into a car that was parked at the curb and locked the door. When their own car came up, the police made a passageway for them to change to it.

Elizabeth's impact on the public is incredible, which bodes well for our movie.

September 29, 1961

Doctors, bankers, and elephants.

Dr. Kennamer left for home amid reports in the Italian press that he had argued with Liz. *Lo Specchio* quoted Dr. Kennamer as saying that if she didn't obey him she wouldn't be able to finish the picture.

I don't think, however, that Liz and the doctor parted on anything less than friendly terms. She and Eddie gave him a beautiful gold wristwatch engraved affectionately.

Now we are being sued about the elephants.

Circus owner, Ennio Togni—uncle of our production man, Magli—is suing us for $100,000 because we supposedly broke his contract for supplying us with elephants. He is also claiming we slandered his pachyderms when we called them wild.

October 1, 1961

Raining. If the rainy season is starting, we are in real trouble.

Burton's wife, Sybil, has arrived with his children and brother and taken a villa. Nice family.

Rachel Roberts, Rex Harrison's fiancée, called me late at night to get a doctor for Rex Harrison. She blames his troubles on food and weather.

October 2, 1961

The location at Lavinia is a mess.

We were shooting a scene in which Cleopatra is encamped facing Ptolemy's troops. Her own army is close to rebellion and she is working on a plan to get to Caesar for help. The location was on the ocean and it was bitter cold and rainy. The sanitary conditions were so bad, the extras were complaining.

October 3, 1961

JLM caught cold yesterday and spent the day in bed.

October 4, 1961

Rain. The studio reports that the film they have received so far is great.

All the film we shoot is sent by air to Los Angeles to be processed and developed. It is then supposed to be returned to us in a week or ten days. In addition, Shamroy receives daily cable reports on the quality of the photography.

OCTOBER 7, 1961

Rained steadily the past few days, flooding the Forum, which is our next scheduled sequence. Even our rehearsals were halted by rain. This means JLM has to find something else to shoot.

Ponza has been scheduled as a location for the Tarsus sequence. I found out that Ponza is a rocky, barren island, so rough we would have trouble getting over the ground in jeeps. It has no hotels, no doctor, no accommodations of any kind for a crew. I asked an Italian assistant to suggest another spot. He came up with Ischia, which has been used many times by other productions. We canceled Ponza and are to explore Ischia.

OCTOBER 8, 1961

Rex Harrison asked for a meeting with JLM. He's obviously disturbed about something. Since JLM doesn't want to take time from the script, I took Rex to lunch.

We met at a restaurant in the Villa Borghese, where I discovered that Rex had done a great deal of reading about Caesar. He wanted to discuss the part and his concept of it and he wanted to be reassured that his thoughts coincided with ours.

A terribly serious, meticulous man and a great artist, Rex, like most of the other actors in the company, wanted to feel a part of the entire project and to believe he was important to it. It was easy for me to convince him of that, since next to Elizabeth, he is our most important player in the first half of the movie.

After lunch with Rex I saw Peter Levathes, who is in town to look over our situation. He is "understandably concerned." Peter, who came to Hollywood from Young & Rubicam, is the kind of man who would be right at home placing an ad for a shredded-wheat campaign, but he is over his head here.

OCTOBER 9, 1961

At last, a beautiful day. Good news from the U. S.—the rushes continue to be excellent.

OCTOBER 10, 1961

Money meeting with Levathes.

Peter charged right in saying things like "God damn it, you're ruining the studio! You have to fight costs! You have to stop Joe! Cut prices, trim the budget!"

I pointed out that back in July we warned it would be impossible to get everything ready by the time we needed it. I also said it was absolutely unconscionable that a company of Fox's experience would expect Joe to write a screenplay and direct a picture of the scope of *Cleopatra* and still load him down with all the other problems.

OCTOBER 12, 1961

Weather beautiful. Rehearsed for the procession, which will be one of the most spectacular scenes ever filmed.

The sequence as planned is long, but JLM is writing under pressure and can't find time to cut. So he is shooting a little long and planning on cutting later. This is an expensive way to work, but we are forced into it.

OCTOBER 14, 1961

Big party at the Grand Hotel given by the Kirk Douglases with Liz and Eddie to celebrate the first anniversary of *Spartacus*.

Liz wore a clinging white gown with an ostrich feather fringe which touched the floor. While doing a rhumba with JLM she stepped on some matches that had fallen on the floor, and they ignited. The feathers caught on fire. Only quick thinking by one of the Italian musicians, who leaped off the bandstand and put out the fire with his bare hands, prevented a new disaster.

Dino DiLaurentis warned me about one of our Italian production men whom we had been having problems with. This man seemed to have relatives all over Rome ready and willing to supply us with anything from elephants to equipment. We suspected that he boxed us into making certain choices or decisions because they were economically beneficial to him.

He was very resourceful. For weeks we wondered how he was able to know everything that went on daily on the Forum set when he wasn't even there. For example, he knew just what shots were taken and when they were finished on the Forum set, which was a quarter-mile from his office. Finally we found he had taken a pair of our walkie-talkies and had a stooge on set who phoned him after every shot.

OCTOBER 16, 1961

Good weather. Finally started with the procession scene, which will require weeks to prepare and film. It calls for almost 6,000 extras plus animals ranging from horses to painted elephants.

The Italian extras are marvelous. They are paid $10 a day and are both enthusiastic and well organized. They work directly under group leaders. By phoning a few leaders we can summon an army of extras on very short notice. On the set, when they are required for a scene, a group leader holding a large wooden stick with his letter stands in the middle of the street and his extras fall in like well-trained soldiers.

Tony Martin was in Rome. He and Eddie started to sing during dinner, and the whole restaurant started applauding, so they went from table to table with a plate collecting tips for the waiters. They were very cute about it. Everyone enjoyed the party.

October 19, 1961

Received word that Lloyd's settled out of court for two million dollars—which doesn't nearly cover the money lost in England.

October 20, 1961

Rain, rain, rain. No shooting.

JLM is finished with the first half of the script. It's 197 pages long and I am excited by what I have read. It's not budget that counts on a picture like this—it's what people see and hear on the screen.

Shamroy fuming about the operation.

Shammy has photographed many Todd-AO pictures, and JLM has never made one before. JLM, however, refused to change to fit this different kind of picture frame. He wants to shoot our picture as a personal story, not a spectacle. Shammy, who is a visual man, wants to shoot for size and scope—with less emphasis on dialogue and intimacy.

During the rushes Shammy talks over the dialogue so much, saying things like "Isn't that beautiful?" "Isn't that great?" that we invariably have to tell him to be quiet. He is interested only in what he sees visually and what his camera captures. Inspiration does not impress him as much as mechanical perfection, action, and getting a full day's work according to production standards.

JLM thinks Shammy is wrong, and Shammy thinks JLM is. Actually, however, they work beautifully together and both of them are expert at handling Liz—they know just what she needs.

October 23, 1961

Beautiful day at last. Still rehearsing and photographing the procession.

I sometimes feel as though I am living in a scene from *The Snake Pit*. Every time I turn around there are grinning, leering, shouting photographers—the paparazzi. They are everything and everywhere. They are like the cats of Rome, hiding on rafters, hiding under beds, always screaming for a morsel.

They were like birds, too, with nests in the most unlikely places. The lovely trees surrounding Elizabeth's swimming pool were alive with photographers with long-lens cameras fighting to get pictures.

Liz has always been subjected to spies. Her London chauffeur during *Suddenly Last Summer* wrote a scandalous story about her. She sued the paper and won the case.

Before she moved into the villa here, the news was leaked to the press, and pictures published of the bedrooms, even the bathrooms.

I suspect that half the servants—carefully screened as they were—are working for some magazine or newspaper.

Bitter because they are not getting the shots they want, the paparazzi report that Eddie is a slave to the whims of "Cleopatra," that he waits on her like a handmaiden.

This brought forth a lot of editorials and mail in the Italian newspapers. The Italian daily *Il Giorno* commented typically, "Miss Taylor must have her children and husband around her every free moment she has. She treats Eddie like a slave but acts madly in love with him."

The American reporters who have visited us thus far have not been much better. They all seek an "angle"—anything detrimental to the picture fits in that category. Our problem is not getting people to write about us. It's getting people to leave us alone.

October 24, 1961

Rex and Richard Burton started their scenes together, and they look great.

October 26, 1961

The new elephants imported from Britain are "jolly" fellows. Doing a fine job.

Liz and Eddie on the set to watch Burton in a complicated scene in which he lifts a girl off one elephant, kisses her, and puts her on another while the mob cheers.

Every two weeks the nurses would come by the hotel and take blood tests and protein tests, then check my cholesterol and adjust my pills accordingly. I am in fine shape, thank God.

OCTOBER 31, 1961

Long phone talk with Hollywood today about the Todd-AO cameras, which hum. The studio cabled back "camera noise" when they processed our latest film, which upset everyone. The camera crew is now working over their equipment. This is a most serious problem.

NOVEMBER 1, 1961

JLM suggests a five-day week so he can have the entire weekend to write.

Elizabeth, Richard, and Rex said they will take a cut in salary so he can have the extra day, but I fear the studio will object. One of the reasons they were enthusiastic about Rome was the six-day week here. However, JLM is terribly concerned about getting the script finished and the strain is telling on him.

NOVEMBER 2, 1961

Liz worked in the carpet scene. Came off very well.

The scene in which Liz is delivered to Caesar wrapped in a carpet was tricky because the carpet had to be specially made of a lightweight fabric so that she would not be uncomfortable and you could see the outline of her form in it.

NOVEMBER 3, 1961

President Sukarno of Indonesia requested, through the U. S. Embassy in Rome, that we give a luncheon for himself and his staff.

The lunch took place today in the Cinecitta restaurant and everyone from our cast was present to meet the President and his aides.

An incredible character who carries a marshal's baton and speaks perfect English, the President soon made it plain to me that he has an eye for beauty. He knows the name of every starlet in Hollywood and is equally familiar with most of the pictures made in Hollywood in the past few years.

After lunch he went on set to be presented to Liz. He gave her some attractive costume jewelry and started to pin one of the gifts on her bodice. I interrupted the President because I was fearful the pin might make a hole in Liz's dress which would show up in the scene.

NOVEMBER 4, 1961

Yesterday Levathes cabled JLM to say he was flipping over the rushes, they were marvelous. Today he called me from Hollywood, upset about the operation costs. He is coming here in a few days with Skouras, who is also panicked about the costs.

Levathes said absolutely "No" to JLM's request for a five-day week.

"We are the laughing stock of the industry; that is the greatest disaster in show business," he said.

When I reminded Peter of the wire he sent only the day before saying the rushes were great, he ignored me.

I was dismayed by his call though I could understand it. We were drawing about $500,000 a week which is a lot of money to be taking out for operating expenses without putting anything back. And none of the pictures Fox had in release or out were coming up to expectations, so the studio was in a difficult spot.

Later in the afternoon Pete called back saying he was going to send Joe Moskowitz over from New York to represent the corporation and be the top man here. I told him that any heavy-handed direction from the studio would end the picture.

I talked with JLM, who is calm and wise as usual whenever there is a real crisis. "We'll just give them the best damned picture they ever saw and they'll quiet down," he said.

NOVEMBER 5, 1961

Received a cable from Levathes saying that under no circumstances would we be allowed to go on a five-day shooting week. He pointed out, as I suspected he would, that our original decision to film in Italy was based on the advantages of a six-day week.

NOVEMBER 6, 1961

Another forty-minute call from Peter about costs.

He is unconcerned over the fact that the phone bill also goes on our budget, as do the frequent trips here of Skouras and himself.

NOVEMBER 7, 1961

Rain. Everyone says that this is the worst weather in Rome in a century—the same story we heard in England!

NOVEMBER 10, 1961

Talked with Peter again, who said he was coming next week. He said Skouras figures our budget at $10,000,000 with overhead, which is just impossible.

NOVEMBER 11, 1961

Here is our current budget, not including overhead. I doubt we can stay inside it.

Scenario	$93,285.11
Director	608,007.30
Producer & Assts.	183,879.47
Producer & Directors Sectys.	27,233.94
Cast	2,622,700.00
Scen. Dir. Cast:	(3,535,105.82)

Music	88,160.00
Re-recording	68,400.00
Titles, Inserts, Fades	50,000.00
Projectionists	2,253.50
Editorial	78,418.31
	(287,231.81)

Art Costs	206,274.60
Set Costs	2,981,992.00
Lighting Platforms	29,052.00
Striking Costs	273,582.00
Miniatures	400,000.00
Spec. Photographic Effects	44,065.68
Dance Director & Staff	60,550.00
Staff	321,266.77
Extras	1,324,537.32
Standby Labor & Material	161,481.11
Camera	140,544.64
Sound	56,706.65
Electrical	396,051.79
Mechanical Effects	135,823.00
Set Dressing	527,532.84
Animals and Action Props	417,600.00
Women's Wardrobe Men's Wardrobe	1,211,900.00
Make-up & Hairdressing	138,771.07
Prod. Film & Lab. Work	250,000.00
Stills	47,600.00
Transportation Cars, Trucks	241,200.00
Talent Tests	2,894.97
Insur. Tax. Fringe Benefits	506,233.04
Location Expense	510,317.85

Miscellaneous	870,033.25
Stage Rentals	136,000.00
Total	$15,214,348.21

NOVEMBER 12, 1961

Nicholas Reisini, head of Cinerama, told me he is interested in taking over *Cleopatra* from Fox and transferring the footage already shot to the Cinerama process.

Now there is a tempest raging outside—the first in the history of Rome. Unbelievable wind and rain.

My apartment is at the Grand Hotel, rooms 57 and 58. Although I face the courtyard, there is, unfortunately, a glass roof over the main salon just outside my window. When it hails or rains the racket is nerve-wracking to me, because I can't help visualizing this same storm falling on our sets. That means no shooting tomorrow.

NOVEMBER 16, 1961

Skouras and Levathes arrived. A six-hour conference.

They both took out after me about the cost. They said the limit now is $12,500,000 without overhead. I pointed out that we had already spent that much, but they both seem to get comfort from listening to themselves, not from facing reality.

Then I told them that I had spoken with Reisini, who wanted to buy Fox out of the picture for their investment. They were furious that I even talked to someone about selling the picture to get the studio off the hook. Later, Skouras got me alone in the lobby and said that under no circumstances was I to mention the Reisini offer to anyone. "It will ruin the company if the story gets out that the picture is for sale," he said.

"You're always complaining that the cost is going to ruin the company, so why not let Reisini bail us out for everything the studio has invested in it?" I asked Skouras.

"You just keep on making the picture," said Skouras. "It's not for sale."

Rogell now made "president and head of the studio," a title Skouras bestows on anyone and everyone.

Later, Skouras saw JLM and said "You're in charge. You can do anything you want to do." Then he told me I am in charge.

NOVEMBER 19, 1961

Meeting in Skouras' big suite at the Grand Hotel.

He called 27 people involved in the production into his room—from the man in charge of costumes, who gets about $250 a week, to JLM and me. He harangued us all on the high cost of the movie for about an hour.

When I asked why all the hysteria, he turned on me and shellacked me for about fifteen minutes, proving my point.

Afterwards, everyone there who was a union member sent in a bill for double time for attending the meeting!

NOVEMBER 20, 1961

To Liz and Eddie's for a dinner party with Skouras, Levathes, and JLM.

What I liked most about the evening was the way Liz handled Skouras. She was able to say things to him that no one else dared; she could make points that we wanted to make, but where he would shut us up, he always listened to Liz. Tonight she shocked him by saying, "What do you care how much *Cleopatra* costs? Fox pictures have been lousy. At least this one will be great—though expensive."

Although he was frequently annoyed, he took Elizabeth's barbs and jests in what passed for good humor, probably because he was aware that she had nothing to lose or gain by telling him the truth.

Elizabeth can always be relied on to be blunt and honest.

November 23, 1961 — Thanksgiving Day

My daughter Steff came to Rome to spend Thanksgiving with me. The plan was to have dinner with JLM, Rosemary Mathews, his production assistant, his sons Chris and Tom, and his sister Erna. The Hume Cronyns were also to be there.

I met Steff at Simonetta's Salon, and asked her to try on some dresses which I planned to buy her for a present. She said she didn't feel well enough to try them on, which really convinced me that something was wrong with her. Simonetta suggested a children's doctor, who examined Steffi and in minutes gave his diagnosis—acute appendicitis. His recommendation: See a surgeon. Simonetta called Dr. Valdoni for me, who sent his resident. He also diagnosed acute appendicitis and prescribed immediate surgery. We rushed Steffi to Sanitrix Clinic where Dr. Valdoni, a friend of Simonetta and one of the foremost surgeons in Europe, operated.

I spent Thanksgiving night pacing in a hospital corridor and praying. My daughters are more precious to me than anything else in the world.

I called my wife, Joan, to report Steff's recent operation. I will never cease to wonder how news travels. Here in Rome it's impossible to have a dream without everyone knowing about it. And in New York Joan had heard about Steffi before I even had a chance to telephone from the hospital.

November 24, 1961

Visited Steff at the clinic. Simonetta came in with flowers and books at 8 a.m. She's a remarkably sweet and thoughtful woman.

November 25, 1961

Letter to Spyros Skouras:

> When you were here last week you complained about a certain unfavorable type of publicity *Cleopatra* was getting. I wish to reiterate that most of its publicity comes from the

> Hollywood columnists that we finance to come over and write destructively about the film.
>
> I have repeatedly asked that we stop sending these people over and the only answer that I get is that another such writer is arriving November 29th at our expense.

In view of our attempting to curtail expenses, it seems to me that when we are getting so much good publicity we should cease spending money to get bad publicity.

With best wishes, as always,

Walter

DECEMBER 4, 1961

Another letter to Spyros:

> I am amazed that you feel that the columnists are very important to our industry. Unless you mean that they are important as subversive agents undermining a great industry.
>
> For years I have claimed that this was the only industry in America that financed its own blackmail. And I cannot agree that a first-class organization should cater to these scandal-mongers who are interested only in increasing their own power by printing scandal and destructive items.
>
> Surely Walt Disney built a good business without catering to them. Even DeMille survived without them. They haven't helped J. L. Mankiewicz, George Stevens, or Wm. Wyler achieve their position. This catering to columnists, dear Spyros, is a myth; and one that is costing you a great deal of money. Each time you send one over he digs up some item that causes us a great delay in work dealing with stars and weakens the efficiency of our operation. There is no way of treating them properly except to ignore them.
>
> Incidentally, nearly the entire group of columnists tried to prevent me from making *I Want To Live*! I ignored them

completely and ended up with a hit film and an Oscar for Susan Hayward.

I beseech you as President of 20th Century-Fox to save the company's money and keep them away from our operation.

Very sincerely yours,
Walter

DECEMBER 6, 1961

Am much concerned over the plan to have Liz work for one straight month with no time off.

It's a practically impossible schedule for her, but it's necessary for us to get on with the picture. There will be just too much tension and strain on her, I fear. She is as aware as we are that she carries the picture. She takes her responsibility seriously and, being a perfectionist, she will be under tremendous strain. In addition, she is not in the best physical condition; the bad back is liable to act up at any moment again. I know she has been in pain some of the days we have worked, but she has said nothing about it and refused to have the doctor.

DECEMBER 7, 1961

Rex crisis.

Rex Harrison had been in England for a few days, and when he returned he found that Sid Rogell, who was active in cutting costs, had changed his trailer and refused to pay for his Cadillac on the grounds that the car company jacked up the mileage. Rex's chauffeur refused to work because he hadn't been paid. Rex called me and said he didn't intend to report for work himself until he got his trailer and car back and his driver was paid. Rex then called Rogell and insisted we all have a meeting in his dressing room on top of one of the sound stages.

Rex, who should have been in costume, was in his street

clothes. He started the interview off by establishing that he was a star, and Sid a production man.

He said, "I treat my servants very well, and you're my servant." After that promising start he went on to give Sid the worst lacing I have ever heard, finally stating that he wouldn't get dressed at all in his costume, nor would he report for work until his car and trailer were back and his chauffeur paid. Rex ended by pointing his finger imperiously at Sid and saying, "You are now dismissed."

As we left the dressing room together, Sid, who was a big man, said he had never before taken so much from anyone, but he admitted Rex had a point. So he arranged to return the car and trailer and pay the chauffeur.

Later in the afternoon when Rex showed up on set, there was tremendous applause at his entrance. Obviously someone had heard the entire tirade and it went out on the studio grapevine.

Everyone knew *Cleopatra* business by the grapevine. It was the main gossip in Rome, and the lowliest extra could dine out for days on his reports of our artists.

I learned more about the "racket" involved in our transportation problem from my driver than I ever learned from studio investigators.

Irene Sharaff's seamstresses and wardrobe girls gave her a fund of information; Liz had her own sources of intelligence and frequently when I would tell her when to report the following day she would say, "OK, Walter—but you won't be ready for me until an hour after I arrive." Invariably she was right.

JLM's contacts were Pamela Danova and Rosemary Mathews whom I called "The Dolly Sisters." Rosemary was assistant to the production manager. Really sisters, they had both been brought up in Europe and they spoke fluent Italian, German, and French. They always brought the news to JLM, who first would say, "Don't tell me anything bad," then in the next moment would ask, "What happened?"

DECEMBER 8, 1961

Andrew Marton arrived to help out with the second unit.

Marton was the second-unit director on *Ben-Hur*. Most big pictures have second, third, and fourth units shooting backgrounds, action sequences, and other film of secondary importance while the director is concerned with the important scenes involving the principals.

JLM had been shooting material usually done by second unit because there was nothing else to shoot.

DECEMBER 13, 1961

Liz does the nude scene.

Eddie, who has been attending conferences because he is going to produce Liz's next picture, is aware of a scene coming up calling for Cleopatra to be massaged by handmaidens. He surprised us by suggesting that we shoot the scene with Liz nude. "Do it properly and artistically," he said.

JLM arranged for the tightest security precautions on Stage 5 where the scene was to be filmed in Cleopatra's bath—an elaborate square of marble with statuary spouting water. The set was fenced in and heaters placed all around so Liz would not be cold.

Only the minimum crew necessary for the actual shooting was used. No visitors were allowed on set other than Eddie and Roddy McDowall, a close friend of Elizabeth's, who had been given special permission to take still photographs of the scene.

The only members of the cast on stage were the handmaidens who were to do the massaging.

When JLM commenced preparations to shoot, I left the set but arranged with our own still photographer who was covering the scene to turn his negatives directly over to me. That way I would have control of the pictures so there would be no leaks to the press.

DECEMBER 15, 1961

Saw the stills of Liz in the nude and they were as artistic as we hoped they would be. JLM felt the scene came off beautifully. I gave our negatives to Eddie so we could never be blamed for exploiting them.

DECEMBER 18, 1961

It was too cold to shoot today—Stage 5 is not properly heated.

DECEMBER 19, 1961

Larry Rice, one of our chief accountants in Hollywood, arrived today to co-ordinate figures and estimate our budget. At least he is realistic: he figures $24 million with overhead, with no second unit and without certain locations.

DECEMBER 21, 1961

Liz is having trouble with her leg, which frightens me very much.

We discovered that Liz had phlebitis—an inflammation of the veins—and she had to rest her leg. The doctor told me that it would be dangerous if a blood clot formed.

I had been planning to go to New York for Christmas but am considering changing my mind. If Elizabeth is unable to work and is ill, I certainly will not go.

DECEMBER 22, 1961

Went to the airport to catch my scheduled plane, then called the studio to see if Liz was on set. If she was not, I was going to return immediately. I was told that Liz had been carried on in a chair—but was feeling much better. So I left.

— NEW YORK —

DECEMBER 23, 1961

Gave a story to *Variety* and United Press that *Cleopatra* will be great and will gross $100 million.

DECEMBER 24, 1961

Talked with Skouras who said there was great skepticism about my figure of $100 million.

DECEMBER 26, 1961

Met with Skouras, Joe Moskowitz, and some of the other top executives to discuss Rice's letter which claimed the budget was now $24 million.

They were frantic. They didn't know what to do other than blame me. I pointed out to them that they had been in the business a long time and they should have known better than to let us start the picture without a proper fiscal, legal, and production organization. They gave us an impossible task and it is amazing we are doing as well as we are.

Everything that had been boiling in me for months came to the top, and I was so obviously right that for once they didn't argue.

Then they tried to place the blame on JLM. I told them again, as I had in memos, that it was not his responsibility to run a production as well as write and direct it.

The meeting ended with their worrying about something happening to Liz. They finally decided to attempt to get life insurance on her, since no company would issue any other kind.

Went shopping for cream cheese for Liz and Eddie. Had it packed in dry ice to bring back to Rome.

— ROME —

December 28, 1961

Went to the studio to see rushes, which were excellent. We are getting superb scenes between Liz and Rex. It is possible to see her great capabilities as an actress as she played opposite Rex.

December 31, 1961

New Year's Eve. Went to a party the Burtons gave at Bricktop's on the Via Veneto.

Liz and Eddie were the guests of honor. Spoke to Liz for the first time since my return to Rome and asked her about Christmas.

"It was the best I've ever had," she said.

January 5, 1962

Caesarion has outgrown us.

The boy we originally cast for the role of Cleopatra's son by Caesar was the son of the UP correspondent in Rome. By the time we got around to shooting him he looked like Jack Dempsey next to Elizabeth. I called California, but there won't be time enough to send a boy from there, so we are looking over Roman children.

January 8, 1962

Rex has found out that Elizabeth's chauffeur has all his expenses paid by us. He wants the same courtesy for his chauffeur. If we don't agree, Rex says he won't work tomorrow. I tried to get hold of Rogell to handle these matters and, in the meantime, tried to smooth things over.

January 10, 1962

Liz ill. No shooting. Peter Levathes in trouble.

Levathes, who was the white hope of the minority group, told me on Monday that at a board meeting in New York on Thursday he was going to be made executive vice-president of the company. At the time he was executive vice-president in charge of studio operations, and he was riding high because he had so many television programs in work.

On Wednesday, however, he received word that all of his television shows had been canceled. At the board meeting he was bypassed for the new job. Skouras was now back in the saddle.

Peter was shocked; his ego and authority diminished. He was also in a very real bind. There was little production in Hollywood of television or films. He had a practically empty studio, with a tremendous overhead at home as well as on our picture in Rome.

Leon Shamroy wants to quit.

Leon said he sees no future in this production, which is constantly beset by problems. The fact is, his wife had a death in her family and had to return to the States, so he is miserable and lonely. This is a real problem, however, because Leon is a key figure. He has an entire crew depending on him and anything that upsets him can upset us.

I sometimes feel like a chaplain at the front line, which is also part of my job as a producer.

JANUARY 11, 1962

Liz is still ill. JLM not feeling well. Sid Rogell is all for moving the entire company back to America where there is idle studio space. Peter Levathes is also for the return to America and is still depressed and upset over his own situation.

JANUARY 15, 1962

Liz announced today that she and Eddie have adopted a one-year-old German orphan girl named Maria.

When she was in Greece with Eddie, long before the movie started, they were looking for a child to adopt and found one that seemed ideal. Skouras used his influence with the King and Queen, but it was the ward of a Catholic orphanage and the church refused to let the Fishers adopt the child.

Liz was upset for months because she wanted the child desperately.

Some months later when Liz was in Germany she found, through Maria Schell and Kurt Frings, another child. After cutting through a lot of red tape, things were arranged. Then the authorities discovered the child needed an operation and decided not to let the Fishers adopt her.

But Liz had her lawyers in America and Europe keep working on the problem. She kept it all a secret, although the emotional ups and downs of the adoption plus the child's illness kept her in a state of anxiety.

When the baby's hip deformity was discovered, friends of Elizabeth's urged her to return the child. She refused. "She is my child," Elizabeth said. "I want her all the more because she's ill. Maybe I can do something to help." As a result, Maria entered a Munich clinic for the first of a series of difficult and costly operations.

It is my belief that Liz sees herself as a mother-goddess figure. Part of her function, in her mind, is to bear a child by the man she loves. Since she has had three children by Caesarian operation, it is dangerous for her to have another child. So the adoption of Maria was terribly important to her and to Eddie.

Elizabeth's own children are with her almost constantly. They are an important part of her life and she is dedicated to their welfare. Immediately after leaving the set at 6 P.M. every day she rushes home for dinner with the children.

The villa where she and Eddie live was chosen especially because it allowed the children grounds to roam and play and enough room. A day after they moved in, it looked like a playground with toys all over.

Although Elizabeth is an indulgent mother who will provide her children with anything, she is very strict with them and they are extremely well behaved. Elizabeth Frances, the five-year-old, curtsies, and the boys shake hands like young gentlemen.

Whenever one of the children is sick Elizabeth spends all her time between scenes on the telephone calling the house and, on a few occasions, remained at home to look after the child herself.

9 P.M. Giulio Ascarelli called to say Louella Parsons has a front-page story in Los Angeles that Eddie and Liz are going to get a divorce.

She didn't quote any specific source but said she had it on good authority—the Roman press. The papers here, on the other hand, are now printing the story using Louella as their source.

We issued a denial to the effect that nothing could be further from the truth. There is always gossip—and someone to print it.

BOOK V

CLEOPATRA AND MARK ANTONY

[1962]

January 22, 1962

Liz and Richard Burton played their first scene together.

There comes a time during the making of a movie when the actors become the characters they play. This merger of real personality into the personality of the role has to take place if a performance is to be truly effective. That happened today.

The scene was written by JLM so that the audience would be aware that Cleopatra and Mark Antony are attracted to each other, although they had little to say—the scene was Caesar's. The stage is thus set for the second half of the movie.

In the scene all the senators of Rome are called by Caesar to a meeting in Cleopatra's villa in Rome. The senators are angry that they must meet in her villa, but they come because it is Caesar's command. And Mark Antony for the first time is seen not as a warrior and friend of Caesar's, but as the young protagonist, the man who will one day take over Caesar's empire and his woman.

While other sections of the scene were being filmed I noticed Liz and RB sitting next to each other on the sidelines, intently talking. Liz was radiant—elegant in a simple yellow silk gown. Burton was wearing a knee-length, Roman toga that made him look handsome, arrogant, and vigorous.

When they were called, they separated for a moment, then met on set in their proper places. The cameras turned and the current was literally turned on.

It was quiet, and you could almost feel the electricity between Liz and Burton.

JANUARY 26, 1962

Distressing news from JLM, who asked me to come to his room. "I have been sitting on a volcano all alone for too long and I want to give you some facts you ought to know," he said. "Liz and Burton are not just playing Antony and Cleopatra!"

JLM is close to Liz and Burton. He works with them all day and between scenes they sit and talk with him, so I knew he was not repeating to me the gossip that has been buzzing around the Via Veneto for the past few days. JLM's concern meant that a real situation may exist.

I was concerned, too. Elizabeth is the pivot on which the entire film balances. As the producer, I do not want her involved in any emotional crisis. I have too often seen how distraught she can become when a person she likes is dismissed or a pet is ill. She was unable to work effectively during the trying time she was adopting Maria.

JANUARY 28, 1962

Eddie Fisher called to cancel lunch because he was going to take his children out for the day. He sounded relaxed and happy.

Evening. Went to a party at Countess Volpi's palace.

The Countess is the widow of Count Volpi, Mussolini's Minister of Finance. One of the most gracious hostesses in the world, she has a beautiful palace in Venice; an exquisite summer home in Circeo, which is where Ulysses was lured by the sirens; and a magnificent establishment in Rome.

The party was held in the ballroom of her Roman palace; the room was designed to resemble a modern and lush night club. Regardless of age, everyone from actresses to ambassadors was twisting.

Although the conversations were multilingual, they all translated into the same thing—gossip. Such parties, whether in Rome, London, or Hollywood, are all alike. People talk *at* each other, vying for a chance to be the center of attention with some new and delicious tidbit.

Cleopatra has titillated the Romans ever since we got here, because of its expense and lavishness, and everyone asked me if it was true about Liz and Richard. My stock answer to all questions was, "I don't know a thing about it."

The questioning was not the nosy, dirt-seeking kind practiced by certain journalists, however. The Romans are realists about affairs of the heart, and they accept and enjoy them as a normal part of life.

JANUARY 29, 1962

Eddie telephoned to say he is canceling his plans to go to New York.

I didn't even know he had intended to go, nor did he give any reason for the last-minute change. I didn't mention the rumors, nor did he. I suspect we both hope it will never have to be put into words. It's still possible the situation will evaporate.

JANUARY 30, 1962

Liz told me at lunch that Eddie has changed his mind again, is going to New York for some recording dates. Since she is not needed for a few days, she is going to take a short holiday in Europe. I suggested she work, because I don't want her drifting around Europe all alone.

FEBRUARY 1, 1962

Eddie Fisher on the phone three or four times.

He said he has heard rumors but he finds it impossible to believe them. Liz is as sweet and devoted as always. He doesn't know what to do, whether to stand by or go to New York as planned.

He loves the children and doesn't want anything to happen to his marriage.

FEBRUARY 2, 1962

I don't know what to believe.

Someone told me Liz was at Burton's villa. I called there immediately, then discovered Liz was at home packing to go with Eddie for a weekend in Paris. Rome thrives on gossip. For centuries it has been the whispering gallery of Europe.

FEBRUARY 3, 1962

Liz and Eddie to Paris for the weekend. Burton to Naples with his brother, leaving Sybil here.

FEBRUARY 4, 1962

A typical Sunday.

I read the London Sunday papers, which I enjoy. Called Doc Merman and found it would be impossible to shoot in the Senate, and the Forum is not ready. Called Eddie in Paris but couldn't reach him so cabled him to return Monday. Charles Feldman, my agent, came to talk with me about a Christmas release for the picture, then took my car to go sightseeing. Doc Merman and Leon Shamroy came in to talk about Monday. Told Leon he must work if Liz returns, which I doubt. Doc had lunch with me in the room and we called Doc Erickson, the production manager, to tell him to stand by for tomorrow. Bob Haggiag, head of UA and an old friend of mine, called to discuss producing a film together, but I haven't the time.

Sybil Burton called to put a doctor on the telephone. Roddy McDowall, who is a house guest of the Burtons', has a boil which must be lanced. Roddy is now in bed and can't work tomorrow but may be able to work Tuesday. Now must cancel shooting tomorrow after all. Called JLM to tell him there would be no shooting tomorrow, which did not upset him, as it gave him a full day to write. Shammy came back to find out what is going on tomorrow. Mel Ferrer and Arthur Panero came in for a session about a company I have shares in. Doc Merman returned to say he was feeling bad. I got him some medicine and insisted he go to bed. Liz called from Paris sounding tired and said she will return Monday if needed. As usual she is co-operative. I told her it all depended on Roddy, and I would call her Monday morning from the studio if we need her. At 11 P.M. JLM called to ask if I had heard from Liz and to tell me that Roddy was unable to work. No shooting tomorrow.

FEBRUARY 5, 1962

Talked to Liz and Eddie in Paris.

Told them to stay another day, as we are not quite ready for her yet. JLM's writing in his room.

Ascarelli says he needs a statement or a denial about Liz and Burton, because the press is driving him crazy. I told him the rumors were unfounded. There is no romance, therefore nothing to deny.

Then I asked Richard to come to see me.

"What's up?" he asked me. "Am I fired, chief?"

"No," I said, "I don't want to rock the boat. You're great in the part. But why do you think I want you off the picture?"

"Because of the rumors," he said. "I don't like them any more than you do—they are just as embarrassing to me as they are to you. I'm a selfish man. My main interest is acting. I want to be the best actor in the world, and I don't want anything to interfere with my acting career. I'm happy with Sybil, who I know will help me in my career.

"I am an independent man, and I can afford to quit this picture tomorrow—I'll do it rather than become involved in something I am not proud of. I will not allow anything to hurt my career or my marriage. And I won't do anything to harm Liz, who is a wonderful person."

Burton said he was so concerned over the rumors that he drove to Naples with his older brother, who is his best friend and confidant, to talk things over. "While I was in Naples," he told me, "I ran into an old friend of mine in the oil business who was going to Africa. He asked me to go along. I nearly threw the whole thing over and went with him. I was going to send you a wire from Africa."

As I talked with Burton that afternoon for an hour and a half, I was once again aware of the man's tremendous charm and sincerity—the qualities which make him a star.

Unlike many matinee idols today, Burton is a combination of the best qualities of the physical man and the thinking man. At 36 he is a very solid citizen and independently wealthy, thanks to wise investments, including a quarter ownership of a Swiss bank. He takes his career and family responsibilities seriously.

He is wonderfully educated, very worldly and is well informed and well read. Some experts consider him one of the leading Shakespearean scholars. He can recite poetry from Keats to Dylan Thomas by the hour.

In addition, he is a complete male. Unlike some actors today who appeal to the mother instinct in women, Burton typifies the ideal lover with the same kind of appeal that made Clark Gable a big masculine star. He has the rugged physique of an ex-miner (coincidentally, Gable worked in the oil fields as a boy) and his physical appeal is enormous.

He does not hesitate to put women in their place. On the other hand, he can be an avalanche of charm. I've met many women Burton has known. He opened up a whole new world for them with his poetry, candor, and romantic approach, one of them told me.

He has no illusions about his own characteristics. "We Welsh are a strange people," he told me once, adding, "That's how the word welshing came into being."

I found it easy to see what there was about Burton that appealed to Liz. There are not many men like Burton around. Liz met him in a moment of loneliness when she was tired and confused after her near brush with death in London and boredom in California. She was, I think, at a crossroads of her own life. The excitement Liz requires of life could be supplied by Burton because of his strength, experience, and the dreams he opened up. Eddie, who is a great deal younger, seems more like a brother.

My interview with Burton ended on a serious note. We both decided that his quitting the picture would not solve anything. What would solve the problem was putting an end to any basis for the rumors. We left the office together with Burton saying he was going to see Liz at her villa.

FEBRUARY 7, 1962

Jack Brodsky, our American publicity chief, told me he can't go into any cafe along the Via Veneto without Crushenko, chief of the paparazzi, sidling up to him and saying, "Mr. Brodsky, just give me one negative of Burton and Taylor and I'll give you a hundred thousand lire [$160.00]. It doesn't have to be salacious as long as I can say it's a shot that was stolen from the picture."

FEBRUARY 8, 1962

I suggested Liz and Burton come to my office for a conference because they are being plagued by the papparazzi and there is no place they can go for a talk. They can't use Elizabeth's dressing room because there are always people there, and if they are seen together in a huddle, it will only add fuel to the gossip.

FEBRUARY 10, 1962

Arrived on set at 9:45 and found Liz in tears because she wasn't awakened for a call this morning.

JLM was very sympathetic and gentle. Everything was serene on set, which means she and Burton must have come to an understanding.

FEBRUARY 12, 1962

Liz did the big scene in front of Alexander's tomb, in which Cleopatra tells Caesar she is going to have his baby. It is one of the finest and most moving scenes between Caesar and Cleopatra; beautifully written, directed, and acted.

Eddie told me proudly that he and Liz studied the part together all day yesterday. Everything seems fine between them.

FEBRUARY 13, 1962

Eddie said he is going to Switzerland to see the house he and Liz bought at Gstaad.

FEBRUARY 14, 1962

This morning Liz was on set, charming and co-operative as usual. But this afternoon she seemed upset.

I asked JLM if he knew what was troubling her. He said he had heard Eddie had called Sybil Burton before taking off for Switzerland.

Later in the afternoon JLM had two telephone calls from Eddie, who is in Florence. Then he talked with Sybil Burton, who has suddenly announced she is going to the U. S.

FEBRUARY 16, 1962

Everyone is concerned about the gossip, which is the talk of Rome and its newspapers. All sorts of fantastic stories have been appearing, most of them libelous, even under Roman law, which is not very stringent.

I went to see Richard in his dressing room to ask him what we can do about the stories. "I'll put an end to the gossip," he promised.

8 P.M. Dick Hanley, Elizabeth's secretary, called me after dinner to say she will be unable to work tomorrow.

FEBRUARY 17, 1962

A perfect example of how the press can blow a minor episode up into a front-page story!

This morning's papers said Liz tried to break through a glass door last night and had to be restrained. When I talked to JLM he said he didn't believe it any more than I did, but perhaps we should go out to the villa and see Elizabeth.

We arrived at the house together at 11:30 and found Liz was in her bedroom being treated by Dr. Coen. Hanley said she was fine but tired and suggested we all have lunch in the dining room. It was a ghastly meal of beer, bully beef, and picalilli.

While we were having coffee, Liz came downstairs looking pale but lovely in a long, gray-blue Dior nightgown with short sleeves. She went into the living room for a short talk with JLM, who soon came out and said he was going back to the hotel to write. Instead of leaving with him I said I wanted to stay and talk with Liz.

For the next few hours I sat in the living room and listened to Liz, who was perfectly reasonable but upset about her life and future. She could not have been calmer. She told me, "I feel dreadful. Sybil is such a wonderful woman."

I said something corny about the tides of life, and how hard it is to swim against them.

"Funny you should say that," said Elizabeth. "Richard calls me 'Ocean'."

Elizabeth said she hated all the confusion and trouble and couldn't feel worse about it. . . . Mike Todd was the great love of her life. . . . She really loves Eddie, but now she is confused.

I had no time to evaluate what Liz said. I realized only that this personal situation could have disastrous repercussions on the progress of our picture. My main concern was to try and find a way to straighten things out, if only temporarily and superficially.

I tried to comfort Liz by saying how much we all love her—

there isn't anything we wouldn't do for her. "You'll get everything you want," I promised her.

Chances are I was boring her with my own feelings and square lectures when all she really wanted was to be left alone. About 5 P.M. she said she was tired and needed some rest. She went upstairs to her bedroom, and I went into the salon to talk with the group there—Hanley and John Lee; Roddy and John Valva; Liz's hairdresser, Zavits, and Bill Jones, an ex-actor who looked after Eddie's wardrobe.

After a few minutes someone suggested I go upstairs to see how Liz was feeling. She was in bed looking sleepy, said she badly needed a rest and had taken some sleeping pills.

I suggested Liz have something to eat before going to sleep and went downstairs to get some food. Zavits brought some sandwiches and milk upstairs with me. She looked at Liz, who had fallen asleep, and said, "She's taken pills!"

Someone foolishly sent for an ambulance, which must have tipped off one of the news spies on the household staff, because the paparazzi were waiting in full force when the ambulance screamed to a stop at the Salvatore Mundi Hospital.

It was such a minor incident, however, that I went back to my hotel to await a call from the doctor, who soon telephoned to say that Liz was fine.

Meanwhile, the story went out that Liz had attempted suicide. My telephone rang all night, with press people calling me from all over the world. I told them the story was ridiculous; that I was ill also. The bully beef we had for lunch had upset me, I said, and it must have upset Liz too.

FEBRUARY 18, 1962

Eddie, who had stopped in Milan with car trouble, telephoned the villa and found Liz was in the hospital. He called me, said he was returning to Rome instantly by plane, which unfortunately gave the press more ammunition.

I telephoned Liz, who was delighted that he was coming to the hospital, though she insisted there was nothing wrong with her and she was feeling fine.

10:15. Picked up Eddie at the airport. He was with Bob Abrams, his close friend, ex-army buddy and business associate, and Milton Blackstone, his agent. We drove to Abrams' apartment. Eddie called the hospital. He was told Liz was fine but Dr. Pennington had left orders no one was allowed to see her.

Burton telephoned from Paris to say he was returning to Rome. I told him to stay away from the hospital, as I did not want to give the press any further opportunity to build up a story.

FEBRUARY 19, 1962

Eddie Fisher called Liz, who wants him to take her from the hospital.

Meanwhile, Burton flew in from Paris and was met at the airport by his press agent, Chris Hoffa, who told him he had been plagued by the Roman press for a statement.

Our own publicity people had consistently refused to give out a statement or denial because that would enable the world press to write a story, "Richard Burton (or Liz Taylor or Eddie Fisher) today denied that . . ." and then go on to recount the gossip. If the press just ran the rumors they could be sued for libel, which is why there has been no big story to date.

Without consulting us, however, Burton and Hoffa worked out a statement:

> *For the past several days uncontrolled rumors have been growing about Elizabeth and myself. Statements attributed to me have been distorted out of proportion, and a series of coincidences has lent plausibility to a situation which has become damaging to Elizabeth.*
>
> *Mr. Fisher, who has business interests of his own, merely went out of town to attend to them for a few days.*

My foster father, Philip Burton, has been quite ill in New York and my wife, Sybil, flew there to be with him for a time, since my schedule does not permit me to be there. He is very dear to both of us.

Elizabeth and I have been close friends for over 12 years. I have known her since she was a child star and would certainly never do anything to hurt her personally or professionally.

In answer to these rumors my normal inclination would be simply to say no comment, but I feel that in this case things should be explained to protect Elizabeth.

We tried to get Burton to deny that he had made this vague, even damaging statement. He did so but it was too late. It was the first real news-peg the press had to print the rumors, and they took full advantage of it.

Then Burton's press agent said that his client had, despite the denial, issued the statement, which added more fuel to the fire and another day's headlines.

FEBRUARY 20, 1962

With the news finally in print I hoped we would be able to get back to work, but I had not counted on the press. The romance is a front-page story all over the world, and reporters and photographers are flocking like vultures to Rome from all over the Continent.

Burton on set—very gay, with a glass of beer in hand. We talked for a few moments, and I realized a strange thing has happened to this canny Welshman. When he came to this picture some months ago, he was a well-known star but not famous; his salary was good but not huge.

Suddenly his name has become a household word. When he went to Paris last weekend he was greeted by a horde of journalists. He was followed constantly. Everyone wanted to interview him. On his return here he was greeted by the press again. His salary for his next movie has skyrocketed.

The romance has become the biggest thing in his professional life. But I don't think he realizes yet that this is not going to be just one of those casual, passing things.

February 21, 1962

Liz sent word to me that she will not work until she meets with Burton at one o'clock today. She wants to try to reach an understanding before they meet on set.

Pat, that blonde I met with Burton in New York, showed up suddenly today. Another complication, but possibly a useful one.

After lunch Liz came on set saying she was not feeling well. "My heart feels as though it is hemorrhaging," she told me—a medically inaccurate but descriptive phrase.

February 22, 1962

When I returned home from the studio today, I found that Eddie had been calling me frantically. "Liz has palpitations of the heart," he said. Just nerves, I'm sure—as in London.

February 23, 1962

Our offices in New York and Hollywood are hysterical over the publicity the "romance" has been getting.

They refer to it as a "cancer" and say it will destroy us all. The press in America has been having a field day.

I have more to worry about than just the "romance," however. Our company on location was like an invading army. We disturbed the Roman economy by hiring so many artisans and extras. We monopolized the Roman press because of the excitement generated by our picture. We were lionized by sophisticated and blasé Roman society because we had the glamour of Hollywood and big money.

The *pièce de résistance* of a VIP visit to Rome was no longer an audience with the Pope—it was an invitation to visit our set. An interesting comment indeed.

We even took over Cinecitta. There were other companies shooting on the lot, but none of them had thousands of extras in colorful costumes. We crowded the commissary at lunchtime.

The logistical and transportation problem of maintaining our group—hundreds of actors, technicians, et al, were immense and difficult. But it was the personal equation, the problem of keeping up morale, that concerned me as a producer.

Some of our crew people came to Rome with only a few days' notice from the studio in Hollywood. They told family and friends they would return in weeks, which proceeded to stretch into months. Babies were being born at home; marriages threatened to go on the rocks; people were homesick and ill. Mail delivery became as important to us in Rome as to troops in the trenches. Letters, photographs, news from home were passed from hand to hand.

And there were the personal problems brought about by the tension of too close association. Our job, plus the language barrier, kept us in our own little ghetto. We were working all the time, with no idea when we would be free and able to make appointments. The doors of all the dressing rooms and offices were always open, with people dropping in at any time to relax. The forced intimacy took its toll in shattered friendships, arguments, and gossip.

As in Hollywood, where on-set gossip is transmitted as if by telepathy to the trade-paper columns, so it was in Rome. The newspapers gleaned every crumb of gossip and printed them every day.

All this tension coupled with forced intimacy was complicated further by constant pressure from the studio. Tempers frayed, then snapped. Key people wanted to quit. I had to spend more and more of my day soothing, cajoling, flattering.

In the old days when I was head of production at Paramount and we had a problem with our stars on the Coast, we used the Long Island studio as a safety valve. We would send our problem people east and the trouble would end. When stars lived in New York, they could be lost in the crowd when they left the studio. They took on outside interests, became less conscious of their own special status. But here in Rome we are on stage all the time—it's easy to feel the whole world revolves around us.

FEBRUARY 25, 1962

9:15 A.M. JLM called. Although it's Sunday, he's hard at work. He said Liz and Eddie came to see him last night. They wanted to go to Paris on the 27th to celebrate her birthday.

I said "fine" but reminded him it is our plan to finish all the shooting involving Liz just as soon as we can. With Liz finished on the picture, some of the pressure from Hollywood and New York would be lightened, because Liz is not insured. If anything happened to her now, the company's investment would be lost. She is even less replaceable in the film now than when we were in England and I said, "No Liz, no Cleo."

All of the pressure from Hollywood, the demands of writing and directing, plus the "romance" are taking a toll on JLM. He is in a state of exhaustion.

He also feels that in order to finish the battle sequences of the script, he must have assistance right away. I called Skouras to get MacDougall back. His first question to me was, "Is this your idea, or does Joe approve?" Skouras always worried about JLM.

FEBRUARY 26, 1962

Liz worked today with Rex in the scene in Antony's quarters.

A good day's work—five and three quarter pages—which is remarkable considering that two pages of filming ordinarily is considered good. JLM is in bad shape, though. He is distraught and overloaded with work.

February 27, 1962

This is the day for birthdays: Joan Bennett, Liz, Erna Stenbuck, and my daughter Melinda.

8:30 p.m. Picked up Kurt and Ketti Frings to go to Eddie's birthday party for Liz—she is thirty today. The party was in the Borgia Room of the Hostaria del Orso. Eddie obviously planned it to show the world everything was all right between him and Liz. His gifts to her were a large diamond ring and an antique mirror.

There was music and dancing, and Elizabeth tried to keep the party moving, and the Dom Perignon flowed. JLM and I left for home at 11 p.m.

I remembered the disastrous birthday party in London last year which probably brought on Elizabeth's almost fatal sickness. What trials and tribulations she has had—the girl so many envy!

February 28, 1962

Now the Italian newspapers report Roddy McDowall is having a romance with Sybil Burton. Such utter nonsense!

Randy MacDougall flew in from Hollywood to help JLM with the continuity of the script. JLM delighted. Randy's attitude is fine. I left them together at the art department looking over drawings of the battles of Moongate and Actium, which have yet to be written and filmed.

Ran two hours and 18 minutes of *Cleopatra* with Randy. What is on the screen makes all the heartache and tension and anxiety worthwhile. Burton, Liz, and Rex are magnificent. No matter what her personal problems, once Liz gets before a camera she's a perfectly disciplined and professional actress.

March 1, 1962

St. David's Day, the great Welsh holiday.

Burton, who had been out all night pub-crawling and celebrating, arrived on set at 7 a.m. and promptly went to sleep. We couldn't wake him for his scenes, which caused a delay in shooting. Richard offered to pay for the delay, however, and explained that St. David's Day comes only once a year.

Eddie phoned in to say that Dr. Pennington ordered Liz to stay at home because her legs are troubling her. They are swollen and in terrible shape. Phlebitis again.

MARCH 2, 1962

Weather better. Rex worked today and was excellent. The doctors say Liz can't work today or tomorrow, which worries me intensely. I am afraid of a blood clot.

This picture seems to be crisis after crisis after crisis.

MARCH 4, 1962—SUNDAY

Rex Harrison called for the doctor today. The clinic is thriving.

MARCH 5, 1962

Today we filmed the bath scene. In it, Germanicus has come from Rome to get Antony to return. Antony refuses to see him because he is so happy with Cleopatra—to hell with Rome, his wife, and duty.

Cleopatra comes in to see Antony, who is in the bath, with three handmaidens pouring water over him and sponging him down while he banters with them. When Cleopatra enters, the handmaidens take off and Antony comes out of the bath looking very chic and masculine in a toga. They commence a beautiful love scene.

JLM's dialogue is right out of real life, with Cleopatra telling how she will feel if Antony leaves her. "Love can stab the heart," she says.

It was hard to tell whether Liz and Burton were reading lines or living the parts.

Burton's friend Pat was sitting on the sidelines staring. Although Liz didn't seem perturbed, I was afraid she might get upset. Since we don't like visitors on the set anyway, I asked her to leave.

March 6, 1962

Liz late this morning because of illness. She went right into a continuation of yesterday's love scene, with Burton's Pat on the sidelines again. Yesterday I told Burton's secretary to keep Pat off the set, please, but to no avail. So I asked her to leave again.

March 8, 1962

The papers today had a story that Burton would never marry Liz. He was quoted as saying he has no intention of divorcing Sybil.

The timing was perfect—we were filming the scene in which Cleopatra finds that Antony has deserted her. She enters his bedroom, takes a dagger and stabs all his clothes. Then she slashes the drapes. She ends up cutting the bed to ribbons and collapses in sobs on it.

It was a difficult, strenuous scene, but Liz did it all with only a few takes. She really went so wild and lashed out in such frenzy that she banged her hand. We had to send for Dr. Pennington.

March 9, 1962

Another heartbreaking day.

Elizabeth is in the hospital for X-rays of her hand and cannot work until Monday. She was too violent when she played the scene yesterday.

Eddie Fisher called, upset over a story by Louella Parsons saying he and Liz will dissolve their marriage as soon as a property settlement is worked out, which is why her agent, Kurt Frings, is in town. Not true—Kurt is her agent, not her lawyer.

The Rome newspapers instantly took up the cry, using Louella as a source, and are headlining the story all over again.

Until the "bully-beef episode" and Burton's "denial" we had

managed to convey to the world press our enthusiasm for the greatest picture ever made. For the most part we had only very favorable publicity for the film. In the past few weeks, however, the publicity has not only been embarrassing but inaccurate and dishonest, as well as voluminous.

James Lawn, the Associated Press man, told Brodsky he has a deskful of wonderful copy on the movie which he can't send out. "Newspapers want only one thing—the Burton-Taylor romance," he told Brodsky. The AP has requests from all over the world for stories on Burton and Taylor. They say it is the biggest story ever handled from Rome, of only slightly less worldwide interest than the death of a Pope.

Sid Rogell came back from a session with the accountant with the news that the picture will have cost $27 million by July 1st. At least that's a more realistic figure than any we have had in the past.

MARCH 10, 1962

Skouras arrived in Rome today on the same plane with Jackie Kennedy. He was most excited, since she asked him to come down and talk with her on the flight.

Otto Koegel, who has been chief legal counsel for Fox for the past thirty years, arrived with Skouras, and we all assembled in my room for the customary conference.

Everyone was smiling and friendly, like duelists before a bout. An hour was wasted in verbal fencing—with no blood drawn, just some deft parrying and occasional ripostes. I still don't know why they came to Rome, but I suspect it will be (a) budget and (b) Elizabeth and Burton. Only one point was agreed upon: There would be no more secret meetings which left out a few of the top people on the picture. We are to work all together as a team from now on in!

We all had dinner with Simonetta, her husband, Fabiani, Princess Alliata, Princess Aldobrandini, and my daughter Stephanie at

George's Restaurant. It was a miserable evening, complicated by Skouras' unpredictable behavior. Sometimes he can be the most gallant man imaginable. On this evening he embarrassed me. He got into an argument with Simonetta and before I knew it he put his hand over her mouth to stop her from talking to him. This to a woman he had never met before. Simonetta was shocked by him, as was everyone else.

MARCH 11, 1962

Although it had been decided just last night there would be no more secret meetings, this morning when I called Doc Merman, our production manager, to invite Skouras for breakfast, he told me Skouras, Sid Rogell, and Leon Shamroy were in his room instead of mine, where we were all supposed to meet.

When they came down to my room, JLM, who had arrived for the meeting in my room, sailed into the others for meeting without us.

Doc Merman and Sid Rogell said they weren't discussing the picture.

"Why do you boys say that?" said Skouras. "You know we were."

During the all-day meeting we were told that there were some minority-stockholder suits being filed against the company. The minority group was charging negligence—Fox had lost between $60 and $75 million in the past two years, according to rumor, and Skouras was disturbed.

The meeting ended when Liz and Eddie, hand in hand, came to get Skouras to take him to their villa for dinner. After dinner he returned to my room and we continued our talks.

Only one good thing emerged from the meeting: Skouras is now talking quality rather than budget when he speaks of *Cleopatra*. He realized only a great picture can save his situation with the Board of Directors.

He berated me constantly for insisting on having Burton

who, he said, is responsible for "all this trouble." I protested that Burton would emerge as a big star when *Cleopatra* is released. "He will never be a big box-office star!" said Skouras.

I said I would like to put that statement down in my diary, which I did—in Skouras' presence. Someday he'll have to admit he was wrong.

"All Burton has done is cause trouble, and you can't understand a word he says," Skouras charged.

March 12, 1962

Skouras, Otto Koegel, and myself looked at two hours and 40 minutes of the picture. They are wildly enthusiastic and say Burton is superb, as are Liz and Rex.

Burton bought us drinks at lunch and Skouras told him how wonderful he was, adding, "I understood every word you said."

"That's more than I can say about you, Mr. Skouras," quipped Burton.

Skouras ended the conversation by offering Burton two more pictures to star in after this one.

March 13, 1962

On the way to the studio today Skouras talked constantly, trying to prove that he, and not the minority group, is in control of the studio. "JLM can have anything he wants—as long as he cuts the script and speeds up shooting," Skouras said. An impossible proposition.

March 14, 1962

I was due to go to London at noon, but at the airport the plane taxied out and then returned without taking off. I'm not very superstitious, but I took that as a sign I should get off the plane. My bags went on to London without me.

I returned to the studio and found Skouras had come in without warning. He said yesterday he didn't intend to go to the studio again. The cast was finished at 3:30 and Liz and Burton were having cocktails with Hume Cronyn. Liz complained of a chill so I called for a doctor.

MARCH 15, 1962

Liz ill.

I went to the Lion Book Shop and bought her some books. Liz is the most voracious reader I know—at least one book every two days. She reads everything: memoirs, historical novels, plays, and the current best sellers.

Then I went out to the villa on the Appian Way to see how she was feeling. One of the servants directed me to her bedroom—the most beautiful room in the villa, carpeted with a three-inch-thick white sheepskin carpet.

Liz and Eddie were in bed reading, the spread covered with magazines and papers. They seemed happy as two birds in a nest. Eddie had just had an accident with his Rolls-Royce—a gift from Liz. Fortunately, he wasn't hurt, though the car was damaged.

I gave Liz a fairly detailed report on the progress of the picture up till now and an idea of the work still to be done. I always regarded Liz as a partner in the enterprise, and despite the unconventional setting, our relationship at meetings like this tended to be very businesslike.

She has sound ideas about script and dialogue and a remarkable insight into production problems. It is at meetings like these that I feel close to Liz. I'm very fond of her, but I chiefly respect and admire her as a tremendously talented person—as a fellow professional.

We are both deeply convinced that *Cleopatra* could be great and determined that it would be great, regardless of weather, illness, or emotional upheavals.

It was this "agreement" between us that enabled us to present a unified front when faced with studio pressures. Liz saw her role as Cleopatra as the ideal woman's role—and she was determined to be great.

March 16, 1962

Once more I had to speak to Burton about his secretary bringing drinks on the set.

March 17, 1962

Went to London yesterday and returned with a planeload of press people who were converging on Rome to cover *Cleopatra*.

This enterprise seems to be so appealing to the world that there is something in the papers every day—its truth or untruth is immaterial.

March 19, 1962

Eddie Fisher to New York.

I think he is ill-advised to leave now. He didn't ask me for advice, however, which is just as well. I was no expert in solving a similar problem myself.

March 20, 1962

Looked at rushes. Was overjoyed with the action and quality.

When I went on set to tell JLM of my enthusiasm for what I had seen, he said Liz hadn't slept the night before and told him she was not up to working today. Eddie's departure has obviously upset her. I called Dr. Pennington and sent Liz to her dressing room.

At ten tonight Dr. Pennington said that Elizabeth cut her eye with a glass spangle while removing her make-up, and he doubts she will be able to work tomorrow.

Elizabeth's make-up, conceived and designed by her, consists of one of the most glamorous eye-dos I have ever seen. To achieve the effect she wanted she stuck a lot of spangles on her lids, which created a wonderful appearance, but it took two hours for her just to put on the make-up.

MARCH 22, 1962

Rex Harrison married Rachel Roberts, a marvelous actress, in Genoa today. We gave them permission to honeymoon for a few days.

Doc Erickson called to say that John Lee, who is Dick Hanley's assistant, called him to say Elizabeth left word not to be disturbed today, as she is not working. A very roundabout way to get the news, I must say.

Skouras called to say he plans to send Liz and Burton letters requesting them to be more circumspect in their behavior.

From my point of view the situation here has improved. Eddie left, relieving much of the tension. Burton seems to have a good effect on Elizabeth's work, which is what must concern me as a producer. Now she's ahead of time and stays around after her scenes are finished. She knows her lines letter-perfect. Most of her scenes are with Burton, and he insists on rehearsals on their own time so that the scenes will play perfectly in front of the cameras.

"You're not acting in the best interests of the picture to send such a letter," I told Skouras. Just when I thought I had saved the day, Burton called me. He was furious. The letter had already been sent.

I telephoned Otto Koegel in New York and told him if we wanted the picture finished he had better withdraw the letter to Burton. "Do not send one to Liz."

MARCH 23, 1962

Eddie Fisher called me from New York. "I miss my wife," he said.

Was stopped by a reporter for one of the Italian papers. "Any new denials today, Mr. Wanger?" he asked me. Very funny.

MARCH 24, 1962

Liz told me if she gets the same letter that Burton received she will quit the picture. "I won't take that kind of nonsense," she said.

MARCH 25, 1962

Kurt Frings is also in town. He complained to me about the letter Burton received from the studio, said he would not stand for such a letter being sent to Liz. I explained my position: their private behavior is not my business as long as it doesn't interfere with a full day's work.

Hugh French, Burton's agent, had dinner with Elizabeth and Richard Burton. When he saw me at the hotel later in the evening he became very excited and emotional about the romantic couple. He wants to make another picture deal for them to work together. He realizes that Burton is now a top personality and important property, thanks to the publicity given the "romance," and he intends to capitalize on it.

MARCH 26, 1962

The news weekly *Gente*, of Milan, published a photo of Liz and Burton kissing on the *Cleopatra* set.

They were wearing three-quarter-length bathrobes over their costumes, and from the fuzziness of the picture it was obvious that it was taken by a paparazzo with a long-lens camera.

The paparazzi, that raffish group of photographers so well portrayed in Fellini's *La Dolce Vita*, have been the bane of our existence since we came to Rome.

Fellini called the intrusive and ubiquitous photographers in his film *paparazzi*—and the name soon was applied to all of Rome's free-lance photographers, who usually travel in a pack and consider all celebrities fair game.

The paparazzi are incredibly patient and well informed. When Eddie and Liz chose a villa, they quickly discovered that the trees by the pool afforded good observation posts. The paparazzi were already installed with their cameras before the lease was signed. They obviously had established contacts with the household help. Every time anything happened at the villa, no matter how private, the paparazzi were informed.

They scoot out from Rome on Vespas or in the fastest sport cars—or drop out of trees onto the front lawn—but they are always on hand.

Although the paparazzi are free lancers who compete against each other in selling their pictures all over the world to the highest bidder, they have a remarkable *esprit de corps*. In Rome they are tolerated with amusement and a perverse kind of pride since Fellini saw fit to take notice of their existence.

Their ingenuity is equaled only by their nerve. One day two priests knocked on the door of the Burtons' villa asking for a donation. Fortunately the housekeeper was shrewd enough to ask them what charity they were asking alms for. She checked with the authorities, found out there was no such organization and threw them off the place—paparazzi!

They even invaded our own publicity department. One of our employees who visited sets frequently always wore her hair in a high coiffure. We soon discovered the reason for it—she had a small camera concealed in her hair-do. Some of the pictures sneaked on set were undoubtedly taken by her. The American crew members try to protect Liz, but we are working with 7,000 extras on some days, and our production is too big for us to use any effective security measures.

Because the paparazzi deal in pictures it is impossible to issue a denial. The photos, presumably, speak for themselves. Unfortunately, Liz and Burton have not always been too discreet, and at times they seem to be working for the paparazzi themselves.

Today we hired nine plain-clothes police to prevent the

paparazzi from snatching any more candid photos on set; we have probably given one or two paparazzi a steady job.

March 28, 1962

A new crisis. The Harrisons vs. Italy.

Rex Harrison went to the airport to meet his wife, Rachel Roberts, who was returning from England after a few days of working in a picture. Rachel was not traveling with luggage, just a handbag. When the customs officials insisted she open the bag for inspection, she became incensed, as did Rex.

They said some things which were not flattering to the Italian government and the Italian people—something one cannot do in Italy. They would have been jailed for the night except for the consideration of the Italian officials.

March 29, 1962

Eddie Fisher is reported in the hospital in New York with a nervous breakdown. Liz called the hospital and found he had the flu.

The "breakdown" story is getting a big play, with Burton emerging as "the other man." All the European newspapers are sending photographers and reporters here to cover Burton, who is the talk of Europe and America.

March 30, 1962

Rex Harrison apologized in court and the case was dismissed, thanks to the British Embassy and our press department.

March 31, 1962

Early today while on set Liz got a telephone call from Eddie, who was in New York holding a press conference. She was busy and didn't take the call.

When the day's shooting was over, Liz and Burton told me

they are so annoyed with the paparazzi chasing them every minute of the day that tonight they are going out to chase the paparazzi!

April 1, 1962

Liz and Burton "found" the paparazzi.

This morning's newspapers are full of pictures of them walking arm in arm down the Via Veneto, Elizabeth smiling and chic in a leopard-skin coat and cloche hat. The papers report, "They held hands, danced and kissed many times." There are no pictures of them kissing, however.

Despite their late night, they were on set this morning for the Bacchus scene. Liz wears a figure-hugging green gown with a low neckline and a slit skirt. Burton wears a Roman toga. They eat, drink, and are merry with a rollicking cast of hundreds of seductive slave girls who dance around them while they gorge themselves on boars' heads, whole sides of beef, jugs of wine, and grapes and fruit.

April 2, 1962

First warm Sunday of the year. Burton and Liz went on a family-style picnic with Elizabeth's children. The paparazzi went along, too, as uninvited guests.

April 3, 1962

Elizabeth under fire of the Vatican.

Without mentioning her name outright, a Vatican radio commentator condemned the "caprices of adult children," which he described as "an insult to the nobility of the heart which millions of married couples judge to be a beautiful and holy thing." The Fox New York and Hollywood offices are wild.

This kind of criticism can hurt the picture as well as Elizabeth personally, so I went on set to see her about putting out a statement concerning the marriage. She said she had been in touch with Louis Nizer, her lawyer in New York. He is to issue a statement saying, "Elizabeth and Eddie Fisher announced that they have mutually agreed to part. Divorce proceedings will be instituted soon."

Perhaps now we can all concentrate on our principal project—finishing a great motion picture.

April 4, 1962

Just when everything seemed to be quieting down, Burton cabled his wife in London. The message, written in Welsh, said, "Love to all. Everything fine." Although Burton thinks he's the only one in Rome who speaks Welsh, the message was instantly translated and put into headlines here.

April 5, 1962

Received the script for the battle of Actium and JLM's scenes for the throne room.

New York wants us to finish with Elizabeth by May 15, if possible. She is our top priority, because every day she works costs us $10,000. Every week she also is given $3,000 for expenses.

Another reason we are anxious to finish with Elizabeth is the insurance—the insurance we don't have. After her illness in England we have been unable to insure her. That means if she becomes ill again the studio will have to carry the cost and this hazard has been their number-one concern.

As the newspapers have reported, "If Elizabeth coughs, Fox gets pneumonia."

Up until today we have filmed 802 scenes and 213 pages of script. The normal average shooting schedule in the studio in Hollywood is two pages a day. Considering that we are on location and at the mercy of the miserable weather, we are doing very well indeed. And considering that JLM is writing as he goes along and directing with the badly co-ordinated production management, we are doing remarkably well. We have more than half the picture in the can.

April 6, 1962

The Italian press front-paged a story quoting the usual anonymous but authoritative source claiming that Burton and Taylor are not having an affair. They say JLM is the man in the case. He got Burton, whom they describe as a "shuffle-footed idiot," to take Elizabeth out to cover up.

Just before Burton began work today he shuffled up to JLM, cocked his head to one side and mumbled moronically, "Do I have to go out with her again tonight?"

Brodsky came on the set to ask JLM if he had any comment about the story. "Yes," said JLM. "Actually, the truth is that Mr. Burton and I are in love—and Miss Taylor is being used as a cover-up."

Later that night, after JLM's gag statement appeared in the papers, I went out for dinner with some Romans. One of them said, perfectly seriously, "Isn't it terrible about Burton and Mankiewicz having an affair and hiding behind Elizabeth Taylor."

April 7, 1962

Burton left for Paris to do another day's work in *The Longest Day*.

April 8, 1962

Lunched alone at Borghese Park and saw Liz with Mike Nichols. She seemed cool and collected and was enjoying the sunshine, the day off, and our company, though she must have been irritated at the beating she was taking in the press.

Late in the day I discovered that Rex Harrison had gone to London without getting permission or notifying anyone, despite the fact that he was told he would be needed on Monday.

April 9, 1962

Talked to Elizabeth, trying to get her to issue a statement to deflate the campaign against her, which is mounting rapidly. She was evasive. Said she would think it over.

April 10, 1962

A very good day.

Shot Caesar's entrance into Rome—a beautiful segment which came off just as well as we hoped it would. Rex, who is back from London full of apologies, was wonderful. The only sour note came from Burton, who doesn't like riding a horse. There were three takes. Richard Burton was angry because of the yelling crowd and the skittish horse.

Another blast today. The American papers have said that we are employing "call girls" as extras. This news brought Skouras on the telephone in great agitation. We had thousands of extras, and of course, it is conceivable that a "call girl" made it into the extra line.

Tried again to get Elizabeth to make some kind of statement to counteract the bad press she has been receiving. *Paris Match, Life, News of the World, France Soir*, and many other European papers are violently attacking her.

I finally called Louis Nizer in New York. He said that, with the exception of the *Life* article, no serious attacks have appeared in America, and he feels the press situation is getting better, not worse.

April 11, 1962

This was to be our first day at Torre Astura, but we were unable to get Caesar's galley into the water because of rough seas.

Unlike most "big" Hollywood pictures, there were no miniatures used in *Cleopatra*. We had an Italian admiral and six Italian naval captains commanding our fleet.

April 12, 1962

The Vatican City weekly *Osservatore Della Domenica* published an open letter which was a cruel and unmistakable attack on Elizabeth.

Dear Madam:

When a short time ago you said that your marriage (the fourth, to be exact) would last a lifetime there were those who shook their heads in a rather skeptical way. We, always willing to believe the best, kept a steady head and didn't say a word. When afterwards you even went so far as to adopt a baby girl, almost as if to make more stable a bond which had no natural children, we really believed for a moment that things could have changed. But children, they say, count little, whether they are natural or legal children, and for illustrious ladies like you there is no child that counts.

"My marriage is dead and buried," you apparently had the bad taste to say. And how about that for a lifetime which you declared three years ago? Does a lifetime mean only three years? And if your marriage is dead, then we have to say, as they say in Rome, it was killed dead. The trouble, my dear lady, is that you are killing too many of them. Even considering the one that was finished by a natural solution, there remain three husbands buried, with no other motive than a greater love that killed the one before.

But, if we start using these standards and this sort of competition between the first, second, third, and the 100th love, where are we all going to end up? Right where you will finish—in an erotic vagrancy (we don't even want to use the word sentimental because that would seem a little bit too optimistic) without end or without a safe port, in which three years means "for a lifetime." It may well be that the next "for a lifetime" will get shorter and shorter to a year or maybe a year and a half, if everything goes well.

The new "for a lifetime" appears to have almost officially started. Here and there remain coquettish displays of a modesty which does not exist.

And your poor children, both your own and the one you took away from an honest institution?

If nature does not allow you any more children, you at least should not go around asking for them, turning them into half orphans, orphans of live fathers and of mothers remarried for the second, third, and fourth time.

But don't these institutions think before handing out children to somebody? Don't they ask for any moral references? In Italy such institutions are very demanding and they do very well.

They do not let themselves be seduced by money or fame, but get down to hard facts and investigate the seriousness of the people.

They can refuse a child to a capricious princess and entrust it instead to a farmer's wife with a clear conscience. These children need an honored name more than a famous name, a serious mother more than a beautiful mother, a stable father rather than a newcomer who can be dismissed at any time.

A few hours after the article appeared Liz, wearing a tight-bodiced, black silk ballerina dress and looking radiant as always, met Richard for dinner in the dining room of the Grand Hotel. She seemed gay and brave. But later in the evening they joined Mike Nichols, and her mood suddenly disintegrated into sobs. She fled from the night club they were visiting only to be hounded outside by the jackal pack of paparazzi.

The pressures on Liz are enormous, and I am amazed by her stamina. The only place where she has any security is on the sound stage, where the crew which adores her can form a buffer between her personal problems and the outside world. She is our star. They resent this invasion of her private life.

April 13, 1962

Filmed one of the most dramatic scenes in the movie and one of the most dramatic real-life scenes I have ever witnessed. Again the parallel between the life of Cleopatra and the life of Elizabeth Taylor is incredible.

The scene filmed in the Forum calls for Cleopatra to make her entrance into Rome sitting with Caesarion on top of a huge (more than thirty feet high) black Sphinx drawn by 300 gold-covered slaves. The entrance into Rome was Cleopatra's big gamble. If the Romans accepted her with an ovation, she had won Caesar. If they refused to accept her, she had lost him, and very possibly her life.

There were almost 7,000 Roman extras milling about in front of the Forum. All of them presumably had read the Vatican criticism of Liz. Not only would these Roman extras be accepting Cleopatra, but they would also be expressing their personal acceptance of the woman who plays Cleopatra.

Liz was nervous and tense before the scene. Irene Sharaff told me later that she had never seen her so nervous before.

Then, JLM called, "Action." Liz, riding high on top of the Sphinx, appeared. The crowd shouted as one, "Bacci, Bacci!" (Kisses, kisses).

I saw the sense of relief flood through Liz's body as the slave girls, handmaidens, senators, guards, and thousands of others applauded her—personally.

Earlier in the day Eddie Fisher telephoned from New York, very upset about the Vatican statement. "What can we do?" he asked me.

I said I thought there was very little we could do, and that it had been overplayed by the American press. Just forget it.

April 13, 1962

Received a six page letter from Skouras today, who was extremely upset about the unfavorable publicity Liz and Burton are getting. He urged me to keep them out of the headlines and quoted at length from attacks in the national newspaper columns and editorials. Skouras noted that practically all the newspapers in New York had headlines to the effect that "Vatican Paper Lashes Liz" and carried the open letter that appeared in the "Domenica."

He was not aware that the letter was from a reader; it was not an official pronouncement. And it was blown up out of all proportion by the press.

Despite all the hysteria from New York and the newspaper criticism of Liz I was not disturbed. As a man who has made a profession of studying the public, I know that newspapers and editorials do not necessarily reflect the public taste.

The American public pretends to be puritanical. But the immense popularity of magazines such as *Confidential*, the peephole publications, and fan magazines belies the public puritanism.

The same studios which require a "morals clause" in the contracts of all employees from stars to executives make motion pictures which glamorize the same immorality their contracts forbid.

These are hypocritical times, when men are permitted to have more than one love at a time and women are castigated for the same kind of behavior. I believe that Elizabeth loves two men. And who is to say that a woman can't love two men at the same time, any more than that a man can't love two women at the same time?

I have lived in several of the great cities of the world during my lifetime, and I have known many women considered to be paragons of virtue. I doubt, however, that many of these moral women have as strong a code of personal ethics as Elizabeth. Further, I doubt that many of them would have been able to resist Burton's charm.

I believe that Elizabeth is envied by most of the women in the world because she follow's woman's true nature—she goes where her heart leads her. Most people don't dare to follow their heart and, in envy, attack those who do.

April 14, 1962

Saturday. Although she had the day off, Liz agreed to work today in the big Forum scene. Doc Merman arranged for 7,000 extras to be on hand so we could finish the scene and move on to another stage.

Soon after Liz appeared on set there was a brisk wind. Caesar's toga began to flap around his legs like wings. Then a sandstorm came up. The shooting was canceled. JLM told Brooks Roberts, a visiting editor from *This Week*, "That wind cost us $200,000."

As a result of the Skouras memo, I arranged to see Richard after lunch. I told him it was none of our business what his private life is as long as he keeps it private. "And stop going to the Via Veneto and those cheap joints," I said.

Burton was furious. "Those places are not cheap, they are very expensive," he roared.

April 16, 1962

Walter Lippmann came out on set today to see JLM. "All that to-do about Liz and Burton is a good thing," he said. "It gets the newspaper readers' minds off the daily world crises."

April 17, 1962

Shooting delayed during the morning for one hour because of cats under the stage.

Italian workmen hurriedly tore the set apart to discover the source of loud mewings. They found a cat and five-day-old kittens tucked cozily up against the framework just out of reach. The mother cat was finally lured out with liver bits, but the blind kittens remained howling under the set. It took another half-hour to get them. At our normal hourly cost the cat and her five kittens added $17,000 to the already straining Cleopatra budget.

An earlier scene between Cleopatra and Mark Antony was held up 45 minutes while the entire crew chased a cat up a wall. The cat disappeared, only to be replaced by two low-flying bats who put on a spectacular aerial display.

Tally: $12,000 for cats; $5,000 for acrobatics.

April 21, 1962

Elizabeth and Burton, who had promised to stay out of the public eye for a few days, took off without telling us where they were going and ended up at Porto Santo Stefano for an Easter holiday.

Since we didn't know anything about the trip, we were unable to provide them with any protection against the press. Result: they were in the papers today sitting on the rocks overlooking the Tyrrhenian Sea sharing kisses and a bag of oranges.

April 23, 1962

Sybil Burton is in town.

She called me at the hotel, quite upset, and said she wanted to reach Richard. She said that, although the London tabloid press has been outside her house constantly, following the children and the nurse everywhere and causing great embarrassment, she has never paid much attention to them because she does not read the popular papers.

But she does read the *Sunday Times*. She saw the story of the Santo Stefano weekend in "her paper," and if it was important enough for the *Sunday Times* she felt it was time to take notice.

So she is here in Rome. She is upset, which means anything can happen. Rather than have her waiting outside Elizabeth's villa and perhaps causing a scene which would delight the press, I felt it better to have her with me.

I sent my car for Sybil and had her brought to the Grand Hotel for dinner. At the same time I notified our press department to try and find Elizabeth and Burton and advise them that Sybil was in Rome.

Sybil was very upset all during dinner. When we were through talking, she went to her villa, leaving me to reflect on what a remarkable woman she is. Sybil is a very worldly, poised woman—and Richard and family came first with her. She was balanced and calm and usually not a woman to be concerned with gossip and columnists. But the *Sunday Times* was a respected Sunday paper in London and could not go unheeded, although she was not unmindful of the publicity that is part of show business.

Midnight. "Liz is in the hospital and will be unable to work tomorrow." The caller was Dick Hanley, who explained that Liz came home by car from San Stefano alone, with a black eye and badly bruised nose. Hanley and Bianca, the housekeeper, brought her to the hospital at 11:30.

April 24, 1962

Dr. Pennington says Elizabeth's bruises won't disappear for three weeks.

Elizabeth told me her chauffeur stopped the car suddenly and she fell forward and hit her nose.

April 25, 1962

The Rome police are investigating her hospitalization as a suicide attempt from sleeping pills. Dr. Pennington gave a statement to the press: "Liz did not take an overdose of pills."

We had a meeting today to discuss plans for the battle of Actium but spent most of our time trying to handle the press situation. We decided to release the story which Liz told me: That the car stopped suddenly and she hit her face during the ride back from San Stefano—alone.

April 26, 1962

Our publicity story got a lot of space.

Liz came to the studio this morning with a bruised face and nose. She can't be photographed.

I talked with Colonel Waters of NATO regarding arrangements on firing the big NATO guns at Torre Astura where we are scheduled to shoot tomorrow. He said there would be no firing. Three hours later he phoned back to say we are forbidden to film on our set at Torre Astura tomorrow. The guns will be firing. We can't go to another setup because Liz can't be photographed.

APRIL 27, 1962

The front page again.

Burton and Sybil went to the airport to meet their children. He neglected to notify us, but the paparazzi found them.

Elizabeth was the subject of more uncalled-for criticism today when Egidio Ariosto, Under Secretary of the Interior, got into the act by giving out a statement after a predawn automobile accident on the Appian Way in front of Liz's house. Burton's car was demolished. First reports incorrectly said Liz was with him.

Sr. Ariosto, who once headed the ministry which supervises Italian films, is now in charge of Italy's national police which safeguards public health, welfare, safety, and morals. He neglected to find out whether Liz was really along and got himself some publicity by saying, "Miss Taylor with her amorous and non-amorous conduct which, unfortunately, morbidly interests and in fact occupies too much space in newspapers and weeklies, perhaps without her wishing to do so, defies Italian public opinion, which has always been very understanding of the sometimes strange conduct of actors and actresses of the film world.

"But I have the impression this time Miss Taylor is exceeding the limits and, in fact, risks destroying herself."

On the other hand, not everyone had such a bleak view of our picture, and I hastened to write that to Skouras:

Dear Spyros:

Dick Berlin and his family left today and I think they were more than impressed, as they will tell you when they see you. I am enclosing a letter from his charming daughter who, as you know, is a student in a convent and all her life has been in Catholic schools. On the way over, Dick said that he thought that through his influence he might be able to arrange an audience with the Holy Father for Chrissie. She looked up at him and said "That's wonderful, Daddy, but do you think you could get me on the *Cleopatra* set?"

Dick told me this as an example of how far he thought the attacks against Elizabeth would affect the film. From this source I think it is quite significant.

Very best regards, as always, to your wife and yourself.

Sincerely,
Walter Wanger

April 30, 1962

Sent Leon Shamroy over to the villa to see if Liz can be photographed yet. She can't.

May 2, 1962

Hanley says Liz looks better but still has a black eye and is swollen at the bridge of the nose.

Had my blood and cholesterol test and I am in fine shape. JLM, ill with a temperature and strep throat, must remain in bed two days.

May 3, 1962

Shooting canceled because of JLM's illness.

The second-unit call had to be canceled also because Rex refused to report for work with any director other than JLM.

Talked with Rex, who said he had contracted to work with JLM and would work with him only. He offered to work Friday night, when JLM will be better. Eventually he agreed to work with Bundy Martin, the second-unit director.

Elizabeth sent for her parents, Mr. and Mrs. Francis Taylor, who arrived today.

Sheilah Graham also arrived. After refusing to see her, let alone talk with her, Burton changed his mind. He said he and Liz agreed they wanted to protect Sybil. So he saw Sheilah and gave her an exclusive story.

Asked by Sheilah if he was going to marry Elizabeth, Burton gave a resounding one word answer: "No."

"He was casual and unconcerned about it [the romance] in his debonair British way, admitting frankly that he is enjoying all the publicity," Sheilah wrote.

Burton told her, "A famous actor, whose name I won't tell you, cabled to me,"—and here Burton imitated his good friend Sir Laurence Olivier—"'Make up your mind, dear heart, do you wish to be a household word, or a great actor?' My answer to that was 'Both'."

Burton candidly admitted that the publicity had hard cash value—his agent is now asking $500,000 per picture for him, based on his new image as a great lover.

"Maybe I should give Elizabeth Taylor ten per cent," he joked.

May 4, 1962

Had a long telephone chat with Mrs. Taylor about Liz and her problems.

The Taylors are very fond of the children and Eddie. They hope their presence in Rome will serve as a steadying influence on Liz. I hope so, too.

May 5, 1962

Elizabeth's housekeeper sold a gossipy story to one of the local magazines. I should say, Liz's ex-housekeeper sold a story.

May 6, 1962

In contrast to the housekeeper's story yesterday, there was a different kind of story in today's *Sunday Express*.

In an interview with Roderick Mann, Stanley Baker, who is a friend of Burton's and a happily married father of four children, discussed relationships between actors and their leading ladies.

> *"I understand completely why Richard went out with Liz," said Baker, who is a top British film star. "It is absolutely essential for an actor to establish some sort of emotional rapport with an actress if any kind of performance is to be given on the screen. And, after all, they had to play some of the great love scenes of all time—between Antony and Cleopatra.*
>
> *"You cannot just turn up at the studio, make love, and then say good night. It's impossible. I always take my leading ladies out, and my wife Ellen knows it. How otherwise could one establish any kind of relationship?*
>
> *"And I'd go this far: if one is a single man, and the actress is single too, a love affair is not a bad thing. Because that way you break down all the barriers—and get the kind of performance every actor desperately hopes to give.*
>
> *"The parallel is the same in real life, after all. One's relationship with a woman after making love is not the same as it was before. The sympathy is there. And it shows. It shows in real life and it shows on the screen . . .*
>
> *"It's hard, of course, for one's wife. Fortunately, Ellen understands the emotional hazards of this profession. And in my case she knows something else too—she knows I'd be nothing without her. That gives her added security."*

May 7, 1962

A beautiful day at last. Liz back at work for the first time since April 20. JLM in good shape too.

May 8, 1962

Months after we began rehearsals for it, we started to film the procession scene—one of the most fantastic ever conceived.

The procession is a key scene in the first half of the film. At the time it took place historically, the world was Caesar's. Cleopatra was determined to have Caesar, therefore the world. While he had been in Egypt, near her, she controlled him, but he left her, knowing that the Roman people had granted him his power and he must be in Rome to placate them.

In making her entrance into Rome, Cleopatra could as easily be stoned by the mob as worshiped. To turn the tables in her favor she decided to dazzle and tempt the crowd by presenting a show unlike any they had ever seen. To capture Caesar she must capture the mob.

The question faced by JLM is the same question Cleopatra must have asked: What can surprise and seduce Caesar and the Romans?

The scene he wrote is a highlight of the movie and, to my mind, the most exciting scene ever filmed. As outlined by JLM, the scene opens on a mass of people charging toward the Arch of Rome. Suddenly there is a chilling blast of fifty trumpeteers mounted on matched Arabian horses that explode through the crowd. The spectators scramble back and away from the flying horses. Clearing the arch, the trumpeteers crisscross in a Cossack manner and station themselves along the road. On their heels charge eight chariots drawn by matching teams. Beside each charioteer stands a bow-man. At the point where visual impact will be greatest, they shoot their arrows skyward. Trailing from each arrow is a long streamer of various shades of warm color. Colors range from pink to cerise, from yellow to orange to vermilion. These arch into the sky and start downward. As the streamer-laden shafts reach the road on their descent, we see through them a group of dancers using streamer poles. By the deft handling of these poles they are able to shoot the streamers thirty feet into the air.

As the dancers flash by, we see their streamers shoot skyward like flames around us. This effect will give us a transition, not for a change of pace, but contrast—cut-away shots, etc. The last reaction shot must be faces that change rapidly from enjoyment to utter amazement because . . .

Watusi! Charging in a savage manner are tall Negroes, twelve of them, carrying staffs from which yellow smoke pours. As they stab from side to side in ever increasing cadence, the yellow smoke-plumes trail from the staffs as the beat quickens. Behind them, six men suddenly raise a golden backdrop of sparkling silk butterfly wings. No sooner are they raised than they separate, and bursting through them into the yellow smoke comes the wild but controlled savage dance of these strange people. The drummers are not there for the beat alone; instead they are an integral part of the dance itself.

The next section is introduced by green smoke, which is made by twelve men carrying baskets of sealed pottery. As they serpentine a few steps, they smash these smoke-filled bombs to the street and green smoke rises. Hardly has it started when a group of sixteen men in green costumes runs at the camera. At the last second they stick their spears in the street and vault into the air, over camera. Camera tilts up, at the top of their vault and from the end of their spears triggered bombs of multi-colored paper are ejected, then burst into a cascade of falling color.

When we return to the parade, we see a group of fan men who hold their golden fans interlocked in such a manner that it is almost like a bubble dance in which we get a peekaboo effect. Then they suddenly reveal a moving platform on which we see golden temples, obelisks, pyramids, etc., around which the winged girls do a dance of supplication. Behind this float is a golden grove of trees that conceals everything. All at this moment is gold, then, on cue, the dancers drop to one knee and fold their wings and become still. At this precise moment, the monuments spring open and thousands of white doves fly skywards.

We now cut to the Forum and we see the doves circling overhead, and coming through the arch, the golden trees which part and reveal the Egyptian Honor Guard. The Honor Guard passes through the arch, the people rush into the Forum like a tidal wave. The senators perk up.

The camera now moves until it is in line with the parade, and above head height. This move, on the tilt up, reveals 400 slaves pulling the huge black marble Sphinx. Every golden rope leads back to the gold shield on its chest.

As they pull it through the arch, women gab, senators are amazed, Caesar is delighted.

The slaves pull the Sphinx close to the royal box and prostrate themselves. And now we see the golden statues of a queen and a boy being lifted by men who seem to be a part of the fretwork. As they carry the statues on the litter to the royal box, there is a silence louder than all that has happened before. At last Cleopatra steps onto the floor and, lifting her veil, bows to Caesar. For a second the silence holds, then complete pandemonium.

Cleopatra has conquered and won the Roman people. She looks proudly up at Caesar—and *winks*.

MAY 9, 1962

The completion of the scene marked the end of Part I of the picture, and everyone burst into applause. Irene Sharaff gave a champagne party to celebrate.

Skouras arrived in Rome yesterday in time for the procession scene. I had a big luncheon on set both to celebrate the scene and to get a favorable turnout for Elizabeth. The attendance was impressive: His Royal Highness, the Prince of Hesse, and his son, an artist who lives on Ischia; Prince and Princess Ahrenberg (she was Peggy Bancroft and is one of the most beautiful women in Paris); Count and Countess Bismarck (she is the widow of Harrison Williams); Count and Countess Pecci Blunt, who hosted Mrs. Kennedy in Rome; Princess Aldobrandini; Countess Volpi and the Duke of Caracculo; Prince and Princess Pignatelli; the Pallavicinis, and the Crespis. Obviously the publicity has not caused us to be shunned by Roman society.

May 10, 1962

At 7:50 Liz phoned to say she was ill. It was impossible to arrange an exterior call due to insufficient time and bad weather reports.

May 11, 1962

1:30 A.M. Doc Merman awakened me to say that he has heard from Dr. Pennington, who says Liz is still ill and unable to report for work today. Pennington recommends she stay in bed 24 hours.

9:30 A.M. Arrived at the studio and found JLM unhappy. Rex unhappy. The schedule is all fouled up again. Same old story.

May 12, 1962

Went to the Lion Book Shop to get some books for Liz, who arrived on set tired and with teeth trouble.

Skouras wants some film to show at the next stockholders' meeting in New York. He also wants a wire from me committing myself to a completion date for the picture.

Sybil says she understands Burton and Liz.

David Lewin of the London *Express* interviewed Sybil and Richard at their villa. "There is no question of a divorce between Rich and me. There never has been and there is not now," she insisted.

"Why should there be all this fuss, anyway?" she asked Lewin. "Because Richard goes out with Elizabeth, who has been a friend of mine anyway for ten years and is alone here in Rome?

"I was away in London, and Elizabeth's husband had left her, and she was alone with very few friends in Rome.

"Should Rich ignore her? Certainly not. He took her out, as I would expect him to do if, for instance, Rex Harrison or anyone else were to be alone in Rome."

MAY 16, 1962

Sybil Burton here over the weekend.

MAY 17, 1962

Dick Hanley called to say Liz cannot work today because she has swollen eyes.

I heard that Elizabeth had an argument with her parents. Her father apparently spoke harshly to her, and Liz, who adores her mother and father, was so upset she spent the night crying.

Skouras is having troubles, too. At the stockholders' meeting he ran almost four hours of film clips (none from *Cleopatra*), followed up by the news that last year's loss from operations was $22,532,084.

He did not read my telegram but said, on his own, that Elizabeth's services in the film will probably end next week. He disclosed that the budget will be around $30 million and said "*Cleopatra* will be the biggest-grossing picture of all time," as I have always said it would be.

At these happy tidings, the stockholders broke into relieved applause, and shortly afterward re-elected Skouras president of the company. They also nominated Liz as a member of the board—and she even got a few votes.

MAY 18, 1962

More melodrama not in the script.

Liz received a letter at her villa threatening her and the children with death. The letter, written in Italian, came from Canada. Although Liz occasionally receives crank letters in her fan mail, we notified the Rome police, who in turn notified Interpol. Three plain-clothes details guard the villa whenever Liz is there and follow her whenever she leaves. A police radio car keeps vigil outside the villa's walls and uniformed police patrol the grounds.

Liz was far less worried about the letter than we were.

Today, at long last, we began the mausoleum sequence. Throughout the picture the mausoleum has been established as a place of great importance. Mark Antony goes there when in despair, and it is the place where the events leading up to the death of Cleopatra and Mark Antony take place.

The sequence ends with the death of Cleopatra—the end of the film. But since the movie is being shot out of continuity, we still have some major work to be done, including the very important battle scenes of Moongate, Tarsus and Actium.

We estimate about ten days of work before the death scene will be completed.

Jayne Mansfield has given an interview to a Hearst reporter, criticizing Liz for her "inexcusable behavior." Called Jayne, who is in Rome. She said she didn't mean the piece to be so critical, that Liz is a good friend of hers! I called the reporter who did the interview and tried to get him to soften the piece. I offered him a "trade"—another story that would have some news value if he would drop the one on Elizabeth.

Then I sent wires to some of the heads of the Hearst organization who are personal friends of mine. The wires were followed up by phone calls. They promised to keep the story from running in America but said it would have to run in Europe since it was already on the wire.

May 20, 1962

Received many press calls over a rumor that Skouras will be out of 20th Century-Fox.

May 21, 1962

Liz and Burton did the "fight scene" in the mausoleum today—and my heart was in my mouth all day.

The scene calls for Cleopatra to slap Mark Antony, who then knocks her down. Normally we would use Elizabeth's double for the action in which Cleopatra falls, but Liz refused the double and insisted on doing it herself. As the scene was filmed, I kept thinking of the time Mike Todd flew Liz to the Medical Center in New York because of her bad back. But Liz, who has great courage and determination, did the scene a few times willingly and beautifully—including the fall. Luckily, she did not hurt her back. I was mightily relieved when we got through the day.

May 23, 1962

Sent a memo to JLM on how I feel we can best bring the picture to a successful and speedy conclusion.

Operation "Home Stretch"

Dear Joe:

In order to prepare and service the balance of the work for you that is still to be done, and to co-ordinate the use of the second and third units, I have gathered quite a few reports that will help us to compile the requirements, questions, and status of the loose ends.

I am submitting these reports to you for your suggestions, corrections, etc. before I organize this "arbeit" any further.

(1) As soon as we get the Actium script, I think we should have another meeting on Actium.
(2) We should definitely have another meeting on Ischia after you have been there. At the present time we are planning to take down 235 people without cast.

(3) We should also have a meeting regarding Egypt.

(4) We should have an agreement on schedule to see if we can get rid of Torre Astura and, if possible, finish with Rex before we go to Ischia.

(5) I don't think we have any problems on costumes and wigs that are not in hand.

(6) The dubbing situation we are leaving, as you decided, in abeyance until you have cut the picture and know what your requirements are.

(7) Regarding script, we are expecting Actium any moment, then there is Achillas Camp before Moongate, and the Confrontation. There is also the question of the Achillas scene to be done over and a decision regarding Cleopatra's Encampment.

(8) Has a decision been arrived at regarding the docks at Actium? Is this to be day for night or night for day?

(9) Another problem that production is concerned about is how to handle the "topo" board on account of wind and light.

The reports included here are as follows:

From Art Department (3)
(i) Jack Smith
(ii) John DeCuir
(iii) Walter Scott

From Production Department (1)
(i) Richard Lang

From Casting Department (2)
(i) Stuart Lyons
(ii) Stuart Lyons

From Management *(1)*
(i) Sid Rogell

Walter Wanger

MAY 24, 1962

Roddy McDowall unable to work because of a broken tooth.

8:30 A.M. Since Roddy is a necessary part of each day's shooting I went to visit Dr. Hruska, the Pope's dentist, and talked his assistant into coming onto the set this morning with all his medical equipment. The near-crisis was averted.

Now a Congresswoman is getting headlines suggesting that Liz not be allowed to return to the United States.

Had a long talk with our publicity department and decided to do nothing about the story, although New York is clamoring again.

MAY 25, 1962

The film of the slapping scene was damaged in transit back to the States and must be shot over again.

Each day's film is flown to Hollywood for processing and showing at the studio. This can of film apparently was stowed on the plane near something which fogged it. The whole scene—the one that made me so nervous—has to be shot again. If it hadn't been for the accident we might have finished the mausoleum scene today or tomorrow. We will reshoot the fight sequence in a couple of days.

Frank Sinatra was in Rome for a benefit. Liz, Burton, and some other friends went to the show, then visited Frank in his dressing room at a party. Something happened and Burton left. George Stevens, Jr. brought Liz back to her villa at 3 A.M.

May 26, 1962

Called off shooting at 2:45 P.M. because after lunch Liz complained of a migraine headache and said she would be unable to continue working.

May 28, 1962

The "death scene" was filmed.

We altered one of the many historical versions of the asp episode. We were determined to photograph a real asp, but it is impossible to remove its venom. We had a trainer from Africa on the set all the time we worked because the asp was, literally, deadly.

In the movie, the asp is seen in a basket of figs just before Cleopatra's hand reaches into it. Later, after Cleo's death, the asp is then seen gliding across the floor.

Although the scene is the last in the movie, we were shooting it out of continuity. I was very upset to learn that one of our publicity people sent a wire to Levathes saying, "We have made it, the last scene was filmed."

I explained that we still had many scenes in which Liz was important, suggested that he come over himself and take charge since he has the authority as head of the studio. He refused.

May 30, 1962

The tension is now incredible.

Levathes is going to take me up on my challenge and rush the picture to a conclusion. He arrives Friday.

With the asp scene filmed, the studio is doing its best to either stop the picture or eliminate as many scenes as possible from it. They have even suggested we use Elizabeth's double in the remaining scenes.

They believe that since we have 314 minutes of film already shot they can cut and edit and make a complete picture as long as they have the one obligatory scene—the death of Cleopatra.

JUNE 1, 1962

The Three Wise Men arrive.

Levathes, Koegel, and Joseph Moskowitz arrived this morning. At 10:45 P.M. they asked me to come to their room at the Grand Hotel.

Pete nervously and self-consciously cleared his throat and said he was going to read me an excerpt from the minutes of a meeting of the Executive Committee of 20th Century-Fox Film Corporation.

What came out was an ultimatum inspired by the high production costs being incurred and the necessity for quick completion of production.

I was to be taken off salary; Liz's salary and expense payments were to be terminated no later than June 9th; all photography on *Cleopatra* was to be halted no later than June 30th; and no money was to be available for the production in Italy after June 30th.

When Levathes finished, Koegel said that I was not to cut and edit the film despite my contract.

Levathes corrected him and said I did have the right to do that.

I told Koegel I had no intention of accepting this ultimatum from the company, but I did not intend to argue. The picture is the only important thing, and I intend to do everything in my power to finish it properly.

JUNE 2, 1962

Slept about three hours, then up and off to Naples at 8:15. Took the *Aliscafo* to Ischia. I went to look over locations where the sea-battle sequences and the arrival of Cleopatra's barge will be filmed.

Ischia, a lovely village almost oriental in character, with white houses clustered one above the other, steep stairways and alleys, is a major tourist attraction. We will be filming there next week at the height of the tourist season.

Talked with some of our production staff in Ischia about the problems they are anticipating in moving a film company into a little island town. The logistics requirements are enormous.

Since our schedule for filming here has been changed so often, we have lost many of the rooms that were promised to us. The housing situation for a complement of more than 75 people is difficult under the best of circumstances.

Everything—the heavy equipment, generators, Todd-AO cameras, lights—has to be brought into the port by boat.

We had to get permission from the local government to rebuild some of the town's bridges; we had to arrange with the police department to police the harbor which is a constant traffic jam of pleasure boats ranging from luxurious yachts to small speedboats and sailboats. For our big scenes the harbor has to be completely empty.

Everything has to be tested in advance, checked and rechecked. We had workmen all over the island, including a crew working on top of one of the mountains building a hut and erecting an enormous window to go in front of the camera. Some of the background and scenery which we require for certain scenes is painted on the glass, as it was in London. Camera tests were being conducted in this location to determine what light is best and what angles are most effective.

June 3, 1962

Returned from Ischia and went right into meetings with the Three Wise Men.

All they are concerned about is when is the picture going to be over? How much more money do you need? They have canceled filming of Pharsalia scheduled for tomorrow for which all preparations had been made and money spent.

June 4, 1962

Rex Harrison called. He has heard that the studio is thinking of cutting out the Pharsalia scene and he believes so strongly that the scene is necessary he is willing to underwrite the cost of filming it himself. A magnificent gesture!

Something marvelous and fantastic is happening to our cast and crew because of all this harassment. The *esprit de corps* and morale have improved rather than been hurt. Everyone except the studio seems determined to finish the picture properly. People who have been scrapping and snarling with each other for the past year have united in a common front. They now believe that this can be the greatest picture ever filmed—despite the studio—and they are willing to make large personal concessions in time and salary.

June 5, 1962

Bad weather, which means we can't shoot our scheduled scenes but could have shot Pharsalia which originally had been prepared for today.

Had a long battle over a memorandum of understanding which the Wise Men wanted me, Doc Merman, Sid Rogell, and JLM to sign.

The memorandum set up new termination dates for Elizabeth's services and for completion of first and second unit photography in Italy and Egypt. Also, a daily report was to be made on the progress of this new shooting schedule.

Merman refused to sign it and walked out of the room.

JLM walked out, too, after telling the Wise Men what he thought of them and their procedures.

Rogell signed and I signed as producer.

June 6, 1962

Unable to shoot today because NATO was firing at Torre Astura where we had scheduled a location. The Three Wise Men have left. They still don't realize that if this picture is great it can be their only salvation, and the studio's.

JUNE 7, 1962

Rained out of the Forum set, so JLM went into the studio where he shot two days' work in one, including a retake of the slapping scene with Liz, which went off beautifully and without incident or accident.

JUNE 9, 1962

Liz unable to work because she has to have dental work on two infected teeth.

Eddie Fisher called from New York. Said he is happy—but he didn't sound it.

Saw Dr. Coen, who told me my blood pressure is up, which puts a strain on my heart. "Take it easy," he told me.

Levathes telephoned from Hollywood to say he had fired Marilyn Monroe. He considers himself a big hero. He reminded me of a time when I was a very young man and was general manager of the greatest of all motion-picture companies, Paramount. I had practically unlimited powers. One day, however, I was impatient and fired a star.

Jesse Lasky, who was my boss, said to me, "Walter, under your contract you have a perfect right to get rid of that star, but that is not what we hired you for. We hired you to get the best out of people, not to fire them."

JUNE 10, 1962

Rain.

The Monroe story is in all the European newspapers. "No company can afford Monroe and Taylor," a Fox spokesman says. No company can afford the mismanagement of Fox, I say.

Earl Wilson called from New York to check on a story that I

had been removed as producer of *Cleopatra*. I said, "It is a problem of cutting costs, nothing else."

JUNE 12, 1962

News of my being "fired" is in today's papers.

Liz couldn't be sweeter. She was so angry she wanted to quit. But JLM and I convinced her to work on for the good of the picture.

— ISCHIA —

JUNE 13, 1962

Arrived here by boat today just as Richard and Liz flew in on a helicopter. The island is at its summer paradise best; the water blue beyond belief, the surroundings idyllic.

JUNE 14, 1962

First day of shooting held up. Liz is ill and can't work. Rogell called from Rome and suggested we stop the picture since we have the ending filmed.

Bill Middlestat, our prop man, was a hero today. Middlestat, a former All American football player and a Phi Beta Kappa, is one of the best special-effects men in the business. Today while on the beach watching some butane tanks being unloaded for special effects, he noticed that something appeared wrong with one of them. He ordered everyone out of the area and, in moments, the tank exploded. His quick thinking saved the lives of quite a few people.

JUNE 16, 1962

Had a long talk with Rizzoli, the William Randolph Hearst of Italy and a big picture maker (he financed *La Dolce Vita*) about Marilyn Monroe. I'm sure Marilyn would be excellent in films here where the picture is shot first, the sound dubbed in later.

In American films, sound and picture are done together. Using the European system it would be possible to make a picture quickly with Marilyn, then have her dub her own voice later. I think such a system would be successful and so does Rizzoli. I will get in touch with Marilyn later and try and fix a deal for her.

The difference in shooting technique has caused us no end of trouble with the Italian crew who don't really believe it when an assistant director calls for "Silence!" Even after all these months our crew finds it hard to believe that we are not going to do the voices and sound later.

June 17, 1962

Sunday. The floating paparazzi.

"Why don't you take my yacht for the weekend and get away from life's problems?" Rizzoli asked me yesterday. His yacht, a converted American sub-chaser, is beautifully appointed and manned.

Rizzoli also suggested I extend the invitation to Elizabeth. "She can have anybody aboard she wants," he said. Elizabeth was delighted. She invited a large group of friends, including Burton; Monica Vitti, the Italian star; Michelangelo Antonioni, the director (*La Notte*); Marcello, the Duke of Caracculo and a pal of Rizzoli's; Terence Rattigan, the playwright, and several others. The only stipulation Elizabeth made was that no photographs be taken.

Since we filmed Sunday morning, it was 2 P.M. before we were able to board the yacht. But once aboard we were wined and dined magnificently as we cruised to Capri. Liz, however, was more alert than the rest of us because halfway through lunch she suddenly looked up and said, "What's that behind the curtain?"

"Oh, it's nothing," said one of the Italians.

One of the party got up and pulled the drape. There was a man concealed there, movie camera in hand. He was shooting footage for Rizzoli's newsreel company.

Elizabeth was rightfully furious, as was Burton. I came in for my share of blame, too, because Rizzoli was my friend. The matter was settled before we got back to land when Rizzoli promised not to release any of the film.

Back at Ischia, Liz thought the matter over and called her attorney Louis Nizer to tell him what happened. He promised to write a strong letter to Rizzoli warning him against showing the film.

JUNE 20, 1962

Haven't heard a word from the executives in New York or Hollywood since they left here.

Although I am off salary and, theoretically, without any real authority I am remaining with the picture and still functioning as producer.

I don't think the executives know what they are doing. Regardless of what they think and do, this is my project.

We are still up in the air about the battle scenes at Pharsalia and the additional scenes with Liz at the mausoleum.

Meanwhile, JLM is going ahead shooting the battle of Actium—one of the most important battles in the picture. At Cleopatra's insistence the battle is to be fought at sea even though Antony is famed for his fighting on land.

On the eve of the battle Cleopatra visits the high priestess of Isis at the portable temple in her camp and asks that the outcome of the battle be disclosed to her. For the first time Isis fails her. The high priestess is frightened—evasive—obviously unwilling to lay before Cleopatra what she augurs for the following day. The fires will not burn. Isis will not respond. A note of doom has been sounded, foreshadowing the tragic end of the story.

JUNE 23, 1962

For five years I have waited to see what I saw today—Cleopatra's barge arriving at Tarsus.

The scene was right out of Plutarch. Cleopatra came sailing up the River Cydnus in a barge with gilded stern and outsized sails of purple, while oars of gold beat time to the music of flutes, fifes, and harps. She herself stands under a canopy of cloth of gold, dressed as Venus in a picture and surrounded by beautiful young girls; some stand dressed like sea nymphs and Graces, some steering at the rudder, some working at the ropes.

The barge was resplendent as it sailed by, clouds of incense rising from burners. The rigging of the barge, which cost $277,000 to build, was garlanded with flowers. The water between the wharf and the barge was thick with swimmers (75 of them) and hundreds of tiny boats. Thirty-five handmaidens on the prow of the 200-foot barge threw out coins for swimmers to dive after while forty other handmaidens strewed the water with flower petals.

We had trouble early in the day getting the handmaidens to steer the barge—they just weren't strong enough. So we sent out a hurried call for some slim but powerful Italian men, whom Irene costumed and wigged hastily. They were then scattered about on the barge where they did the actual work while the beautiful girls merely functioned as props.

This is also Liz's last day on the picture according to executive order of the studio.

The press wanted a story but we feared that if it was announced that Liz was finished in the picture it could be the signal for the press to descend again. Liz was determined to stay with the picture as long as possible.

Since we wanted to keep everyone happy we put out a story that it was not Liz's last day, that she was finished for the moment but we expected to use her in other scenes.

JUNE 25, 1962

My lawyer, Greg Bautzer, says I am to remain on the job as producer. He will get Fox to put out an announcement to that effect.

JUNE 26, 1962

Skouras has resigned from Fox, to become effective September 20, 1962.

James Aubrey, President of CBS-TV's network division and Darryl F. Zanuck are being mentioned as possibilities to take over.

Darryl, who is an old and good friend of mine, was production chief for many years and, in addition, is the company's largest single stockholder.

Although I have spent much of my time the past few years fighting with Skouras I was sorry to learn he was resigning. Despite our many differences of opinion, I had always considered Skouras one of the best showmen in the business. He could have done a good job of selling *Cleopatra*, and had some novel ideas of getting guarantees before it opens.

JUNE 28, 1962

Hume Cronyn finished his final scene as Sosigones today.

Hume was in full costume on the pier when the scene ended. He called to JLM, "Is that all, Joe?"

"Yes, Hume," JLM said.

Hume turned to his wife, Jessica Tandy, who was on the sidelines watching, and shouted, "Jessie, we'll go home." With that he leaped happily off the pier into the water 25 feet below.

JUNE 29, 1962

Now New York wants to call off Philippi—another scene which they never before have hinted they'd like to kill. The set is under construction and it's ridiculous to do away with it, as the scene is essential for the opening of the second part of the film.

Obviously, New York cares about just one thing—ending the picture regardless of how and despite the fact we have only three weeks more to go.

JLM is so upset he sent the following cable to Skouras, Levathes, and Judge Rosenman:

> WITHOUT PHARSALIA IN MY OPINION OPENING OF FILM AND FOLLOWING SEQUENCES SEVERELY DAMAGED STOP BUT WITHOUT PHILIPPI THERE IS LITERALLY NO OPENING FOR SECOND HALF SINCE INTERIOR TENT SCENES ALREADY SHOT SIMPLY CANNOT BE INTELLIGIBLY PUT TOGETHER STOP . . . FOR MY PART I HAVE EXHAUSTED SUCH ENERGIES AND TALENT AS I POSSESS AND THE PROSPECT OF A FLOW OF SIMILAR PRONUNCIAMENTOS IN THE MONTH AHEAD IS ONE I CANNOT FACE STOP NOR WOULD I WANT TO FACE THE FILM I COULD NOT ASSEMBLE PROPERLY MUCH LESS TURN OVER WITH PRIDE STOP WITH MUTUAL APPRECIATION OF RESPONSIBILITIES AND SUGGESTING THAT MINE TOWARD THE STOCKHOLDERS IS NO LESS THAN YOURS I SUGGEST THAT YOU REPLACE ME SOONEST POSSIBLE BY SOMEONE LESS CRITICAL OF YOUR DIRECTIVES AND LESS DEDICATED TO THE EVENTUAL SUCCESS OF CLEOPATRA.
>
> JOSEPH L. MANKIEWICZ

June 30, 1962

Zanuck is in the fray—and he makes good sense.

Darryl, who is now in New York, gave the press a statement representing a complete vote of confidence in Skouras' regime and an equally complete indictment of Fox's "rule by committee" which, he said, "has approved all major decisions in production and administration during the last several years."

Although DFZ did not say whether he had been offered the presidency of Fox, he said that the company's president "must have the unqualified and unanimous support of a unified board of directors. He need not necessarily have total autonomy, but to function properly . . . he cannot be placed in a position where he is 'second guessed' by inexperienced 'committees' . . ." By which he means committees loaded with Wall Street directors.

DFZ's statement placed him smack in the middle of the factional fight within the studio's board as to who will succeed Spyros. I think DFZ may be the man we are hoping for. Although his recent record as a producer is not good (most of his pictures lost money) he has a good record as a studio head and should be in Hollywood.

July 1, 1962

Sunday. The Italian crew refused to work today and I must say they are right.

Along with our American crew the Italians have been working days and nights all week long; most of them sleep in their clothes near the set at Ischia. Doc Merman has done a magnificent job prodding them. But we have been driving them too hard in order to finish here quickly, so they insisted on a day off.

July 2, 1962

Still no firm stand on Egypt.

One day we are going to shoot there, commitments are made, schedules planned. The next day Egypt is called off and we are to shoot the battle sequences in Spain and/or the United States.

July 5, 1962

Egypt is back on the schedule. We are returning to Rome to get ready.

— ROME —

July 7, 1962

Cable from Liz's lawyer Martin Gang.

LEVATHES REFUSED TO REVOKE ORDERS TERMINATING ITALIAN PRODUCTION CLAIMS MAUSOLEUM SCENES NOT NEEDED PHARSALIA TOO EXPENSIVE

JULY 9, 1962

Liz wants to go to Egypt with the company but Doc Merman, who has talked with some of our Egyptian production people, says definitely not.

He was told that if she goes to Egypt there is a good chance she will be killed or there will be riots, because when she was married to Eddie Fisher, Liz made a large contribution to Israeli charities. Sounds ridiculous and improbable but Merman is convinced it would be dangerous for her.

JULY 11, 1962

Woke up tired on my 68th birthday.

Felt better after a visit with my doctor, who said I am in good health. Surprisingly, I am one of the few people on the film who hasn't been sick a day.

We leave for Egypt on the 15th.

JULY 14, 1962

Up early and dictated a letter to Jerry Wald. At 8 A.M. I got a call from Giulio saying Jerry had died last night. A terrible blow. Jerry was a wonderful character, a great friend and he loved making movies. The rest of the day was gloomy.

— ALEXANDRIA —

JULY 15, 1962

Settled in at the Hotel Salamlek-Montazah, one of Farouk's old palaces.

Alexandria is just as Lawrence Durrell described it in *Justine*—"long sequences of tempera. Light filtered through the essence of lemons. An air full of brick-dust—sweet smelling brick dust and the odour of hot pavements slaked with water. Light damp clouds, earth bound yet seldom bringing rain. Upon this squirt dust-red, dusty-green, chalk-mauve and watered crimson lake. In summer the sea damp lightly varnished the air. Everything lay under a coat of gum. . . ."

JULY 17, 1962

Confusion and misrepresentation as always.

One of the reasons we decided to come to Egypt was the government's promise that we could have 5,000 soldiers of the Egyptian Army at $1 per man per day. When Doc Merman arrived here he met with a general who said nothing was settled yet and tried to raise the price to $4 a soldier. Doc is now trying to make arrangements to use local townspeople as extras in the battle sequence, which we always felt would be the eventual method of working.

None of our equipment—generators, trucks, jeeps, etc.—has arrived as scheduled yet. The costumes are not here nor are the barges, and we are scheduled to start shooting tomorrow!

JULY 18, 1962

7 A.M. Left for Edkou, a small and primitive village about an hour outside of Alexandria, where we shot one brief scene with Burton, then returned to the hotel for a production meeting.

General confusion: no manifests, Misair didn't deliver the make-up and wigs required for tomorrow, the ships haven't delivered the cargo needed tomorrow, twelve promised jeeps are nowhere in sight, our equipment is failing, trucks breaking down. It's hot and everyone's nerves are frayed to the breaking point.

July 20, 1962

No shooting.

Yesterday I got Fahti to call the Vice President of Egypt, who ordered customs to remain open all day for us, a major concession as Friday is normally a holiday here.

Today, after an intensive drive to get a special case to location it proved to be the wrong one. It was mislabeled. In addition, much of our equipment and wardrobe was shipped from Naples here on one ship in order to save time. Everything was carefully marked so it could be found, but when the ship got to Alexandria the crane broke down. Since the ship had a schedule it took off—with most of our equipment—for Beirut. Now we have to wait four days for the ship to return.

July 21, 1962

The extras rioted.

When Doc Merman found he was unable to make a deal with the Egyptian government for soldiers he arranged with a local agent to deliver extras to the location at Edkou for $4 a head. For today's scene we needed about 5,000 extras including 1,500 light-skinned Egyptians who were to be Romans.

The agent imported 750 students from the universities at Alexandria. When they arrived on the set, the local people rioted—guns, clubs, and rocks. The locals refused to work with the Alexandrians.

The riot overran the twenty or so Egyptian army men and police on set but, happily, it was quelled instantly when three camel-corps men appeared on the scene.

July 22, 1962

More riots and confusion, with everyone behaving like Beau Geste just before the big blowup.

Our living conditions are difficult. We sleep under nets because of the bugs. There are scorpions in the location and sand gets into everything. We have no privacy—even the telephone calls are monitored.

The Egyptian papers had a big story today about a telephone call Burton placed to Liz in Rome two days ago. He told her in detail of the hardships we are facing. She told him with equal color how she feels about the Egyptians refusing to let her into the country—and what they can do with their country.

Despite the hardships and confusion and problems, we are proceeding on schedule with the filming. Our crew is wonderful.

July 23, 1962

JLM is suffering from exhaustion and with good reason. He has something wrong with his leg and is walking with a stick I gave him.

The biggest scenes have been filmed, despite the most incredible hardships plus laziness on the part of the extras. We noticed one of our horsemen in the distance in a scene wearing a uniform that was outrageously big. When the horseman was called in to find out what the trouble was, we found it was the nine year old son of one of the extras. His father who was asleep nearby under a tree had put his son in the uniform, then mounted him on the horse and sent him in to work.

Tomorrow will see the end of Egypt and—I hope—the end of the picture for the first unit.

July 24, 1962

JLM still ill. Shamroy is having blood-pressure trouble. One of the horses threw a rider, who was hurt.

By the end of the day, we finished the location shooting with the first unit, however, which meant that most of us were finished with the picture. We returned in the evening to Alexandria where Fahti and the San Stefano Hotel were hosts at a party for the cast and crew in the main dining room.

This was the last time that many of us would see one another again, and the wine and the occasion made for a surprising sentiment. I was glad that the picture was finally over but sorry, too. It had been four hard years, but while the picture was being made it was my life.

Everyone was called on to make a speech. Most of them were like Oscar acceptance speeches—interminable lists of credits and thanks.

What my own speech lacked in content it made up for in heartfelt emotion. "Tonight we are gathered here, within hours of completing the greatest attraction in the history of entertainment," I said. "I wish I could give you all the reward you deserve—a Presidential Citation to the entire company would not be too much.

"From the dark days of our Dunkirk in London, when Sir Winston Mankiewicz with brave leadership and wisdom guided us to safety through seas infested with wolf packs of submarines from the New York office, of U-2 bombs from Hollywood, he never wavered in his desire to make this the biggest and best picture.

"I want to pay tribute to Queen Elizabeth, the reigning monarch of the screen, a woman of character and a fighter for ideals. And, I salute that great Welsh hero, St. David Burton, who has won all of our hearts and who is destined to startle the world with his dynamic performance. Tribute also to Rex Caesar Emperatur Emperata whose magnificent, sincere performance has thrilled us all. And to Roddy McDowall's brilliant Octavian.

"I also want to pay my respect and gratitude to those who made all this possible—the magnificent infantry of 20th Century-Fox's back lot; the artisans and technicians who met every situation; Leon Shamroy and his great crew, Freddy Simpson and his flame throwers; Irene Sharaff, who never missed a date through the long experience and during problems that have never been equaled in the history of Hollywood.

"We've had our defeats and dark moments but the light was

always ahead. And when it looked as if the enemy was going to win, Field Marshal Montgomery Merman appeared at our Alamein with General Ike Erickson, and the tide was stemmed by Monty Merman's hat and picturesque language and Ike Erickson's calm and character.

"I wish I had time to tell you how much we are in debt to LaBella's raiders, to Middlestat's Marauders, to Jack Tait, Herb Cheek's Shock Troops, Bundy Martin's Reserves, Stuart Lyons' handmaidens, Leo McCarey, Gilly, Ted Hall Moeller, Rosenberg, Rosemary Mathews, John DeCuir, Walter Scott, Eddie Wynigear—all capable soldiers. Each and every one of you deserves recognition for service beyond the call of duty, as do hundreds of others I don't have time to mention. From the bottom of my heart I want to thank you all."

It was a corny speech, but I meant every word of it.

FADE OUT

EPILOGUE

— NEW YORK —

March 7, 1963

It would be pleasant to say that the trials and tribulations which characterized the making of *Cleopatra* ended with that day in Egypt eight months ago when I made my farewell speech. It would also be pleasant to say that the pleasures of fame and fortune made all our sufferings worth while and, that in the true Hollywood tradition, we lived happily thereafter. The truth is something else again.

A few weeks after we finished in Egypt, Darryl F. Zanuck was made president of 20th Century-Fox. He promptly terminated JLM's services as director because, Zanuck said, Joe demanded full control over *Cleopatra*, a right Zanuck felt must be reserved for himself as president of the studio.

Ironically, Zanuck, who had earlier blamed "committee mismanagement" for the high cost of *Cleopatra*, reversed his stand once he came in as president of the studio. He blamed JLM for the high cost of the film.

When the smoke of charge and counter-charge cleared last month, Zanuck reversed himself again and reinstated JLM to rewrite and direct our additional scenes. As I write this, JLM has just completed filming in Madrid the Philippi and Pharsalia battle scenes—the same episodes which brought about our crises in Rome last June when the old management killed the scenes, saying there was not money enough for them. I am delighted for this vindication of our original script.

But this belated acceptance of our original program has caused an estimated $2 million to be added to our towering budget. The total cost of *Cleopatra* is now approximately $37 million.

The studio, following a plan outlined by Skouras a year ago, has already begun to sell *Cleopatra* to the public. People are lined up in New York to buy tickets. At this writing eighteen theaters have already guaranteed Fox $11.5 million on the picture—the largest advance exhibition contracts in entertainment history. From every indication it looks as if the picture will perform the miracle of making a big profit.

In a recent interview, Darryl F. Zanuck told the *Wall Street Journal* that Fox would break even with a gross of approximately $62 million. In reply to a question, he said he didn't believe it is "impossible" for the film to gross $100 million world-wide in its initial run—the same estimate I made in December 1961, long before the picture was finished.

Meanwhile, what of the people who made the movie and whose lives form such an integral part of my story?

Spyros Skouras, who once ruled Fox with an iron hand and a Greek bellow, still sits at a big desk in Fox's 56th Street offices—but only on Zanuck's tolerance. Skouras' bellow has been reduced to a whisper, but I believe there is plenty of fight in him yet.

Eddie Fisher has resumed his career and is successful again on records and in night clubs. He still loves Liz, just as I am sure she loves him.

Elizabeth and Burton are now in London making *Very Important Persons*, a modest-budget film in which they are partners, and which MGM is rushing to completion to capitalize on their tremendous publicity.

Thanks to Elizabeth and *Cleopatra*, Burton has become a

very big star. His salary has more than tripled in the past two years.

As for Elizabeth, one thing is certain: she is made of far sterner stuff than most of us. When the day comes that she knows what she really wants from life, she will—I am sure—get it.

During the year *Cleopatra* was in production I watched Liz mature as an actress as well as a woman. I have nothing but admiration for the way she stood up under fire for her personal and professional beliefs. It is to her credit that despite unprecedented personal criticism she has emerged as the most important star in motion pictures today. The same publications which chastise her in print put her picture on the cover to sell copies—a blatant form of hypocrisy.

The fact is that everyone everywhere is interested in Elizabeth. It is not a far stretch of the imagination to compare Elizabeth with Cleopatra. She has the intelligence and temperament of the Egyptian Queen—and she has the honesty and directness that characterize all big people.

She also has one other thing that sets her apart from any other woman today—the most outstanding talent I have seen in any actress in the past generation.

When Elizabeth and I began *Cleopatra* four years ago, we hoped it would be a great motion picture, one the world would be excited over. I feel we have achieved our goal. There will never be another motion picture like *Cleopatra*, just as there never was another woman like her—or Elizabeth.

AFTERWORD

It was, and remains to this day, a film drenched in superlatives. It was called the most publicized movie of all time, the most expensive, the most reviled, even, at its 4 hour and 3 minute original theatrical cut, the longest film Hollywood ever released. Its star, Elizabeth Taylor, received the highest salary ever for an actress, a million dollars plus 10 per cent of the gross, and threw up the first time she saw it. Her celebrated costar, Richard Burton, claimed never to have seen it at all. It could only be *Cleopatra*.

It's been fifty years since *Cleopatra* premiered on a June night in 1963 at New York's Rivoli Theater, an event that both required the services of more than 100 policemen, the largest group ever assigned to a Broadway opening, and caused beleaguered writer-director Joseph L. Mankiewicz to feel like he was being carted to the guillotine in a tumbrel.

In that half a century, other films have caused a fuss and salaries and budgets have gone so sky high that *Cleopatra*'s once astronomical cost (estimates range from $32 million to $44 million) now seems almost quaint by comparison.

But *Cleopatra* still lingers in memory and legend, a cultural milestone whose significance is not exactly clear. It is not often revived these days and rarely reconsidered. While other epics once viewed as fiascos, like Michael Cimino's *Heaven's Gate*, have maneuvered their way from purgatory to critical respectability, time has so stood still for *Cleopatra* that seeing it again feels like a trip back to the waning days of a formidable empire. Not the last days of Egypt's greatness, but of Hollywood's.

For the key thing that remains a constant about *Cleopatra* is that it's still difficult to watch without the real world intruding. Even now the fuss and the film remain so fatally intertwined, like Holmes and Moriarty headed over Reichenbach Falls, that separating one from the other is challenging and perhaps not even necessary. Because the things that gave *Cleopatra* notoriety in its day remain the qualities that fascinate today.

Key among those aspects was the enormous, still-impressive physical scale of the film, the huge number of objects that in those pre-CGI days were actually built by hand. These included the construction of an authentic harbor, a twelve-acre Roman Forum set bigger than the actual Forum, and a royal barge built to Plutarch's specifications that almost ended up as a restaurant at the 1964 New York World's Fair.

Not to mention (though everyone did) the 26,000 gallons of paint, 6,000 tons of cement, 150,000 arrows, 8,000 pairs of shoes, and 26,000 costumes. These clothes weren't all for Cleopatra herself, though it sometimes seemed they were: the queen had only 58 costumes, including one of pure gold that cost $6,500 back in the day. All in all, the physical Cleopatra still impresses as the last gaudy gasp of a way of Hollywood life that rising costs and shrinking audiences were bringing to an end.

It was not just the physical backdrop, of course, that remains compelling about *Cleopatra*, it's the legendary romantic liaison between Taylor, Hollywood's biggest star, and Burton, called by actress Jean Simmons "an enviable cross between Groucho Marx and John Barrymore." It was a stormy relationship that lasted more than a dozen years and included two marriages and two divorces. Its specifics never ceased to captivate the world because it both began during filming and echoed in uncanny ways the story the film itself was telling.

Moviegoers invested in what's seen on the big screen like

nothing better than being told that the emotions they're watching are duplicating reality. Audiences were enthralled when Greta Garbo and John Gilbert fell in love while making 1926's *Flesh and the Devil*, and Burton-Taylor upped the ante in a way that remains potent today.

Cleopatra is more than life imitating art, it's life and art feeding on and changing each other. The lovers dallied as the world's press salivated. Things got so intense that Vatican City's weekly newspaper ran an open letter accusing Taylor of "erotic vagrancy" and Hedda Hopper reported that studio executives were rooting for astronaut John Glenn's Project Mercury flight to make it into earth's orbit and finally kick the potent, passionate liaison off newspaper front pages.

That this film exists at all is due to a passion of a different sort, a lifelong dream of Walter Wanger, a prolific producer whose Hollywood experience goes all the way back to purchasing the property that became 1921's Rudolph Valentino-starring *The Sheik*. His idea, as related in the film's substantial souvenir program, was a motion picture "that would interpret, more realistically than ever done before, Cleopatra's life and the era in which she lived."

Rather than ask what went wrong with that dream, it's more instructive to say "What didn't?" The film was bedeviled from the get-go by all manner of ills, from dreadful weather and a hairdressers' strike in England (the production site before Rome) to several Taylor illnesses, including one that nearly killed her but led to a sympathy Oscar for *Butterfield 8*, as well as a director, Rouben Mamoulian, who was better at spending money than creating usable footage.

Partially at Taylor's suggestion, Mankiewicz, whose credits included *All About Eve* and *The Barefoot Contessa* and had worked with the actress on *Suddenly, Last Summer*, took over to both write and direct. The trouble was the budget-driven necessity, aided by pills and injections, to do both almost simultaneously, shooting by day and writing by night.

The result, as the filmmaker sardonically related in Kenneth L. Geist's *Pictures Will Talk: The Life and Films of Joseph L. Mankiewicz*, was "the hardest three pictures I ever made . . . *Cleopatra* was conceived in emergency, shot in hysteria, and wound up in blind panic."

In an atmosphere like this, everything that could become a crisis did. When the filmmakers changed their minds about using a group of elephants, their owner insisted the animals had been "slandered" and decided to sue. And when eleven U.S. Congressmen found a reason to visit the set in Rome and Taylor didn't find time to meet with them, the resulting story ("Film Set Snub Irks Visiting Congressmen") became an international incident.

It is a shock after all of this silliness to discover how serious the intentions for *Cleopatra* were. Mankiewicz was nothing if not a thoughtful, adult filmmaker, and his aim here, which fit nicely with Wanger's, was to create what the producer described as a "modern, psychiatrically rooted concept" that dealt with the complex personal relationships between mentor Julius Caesar, protégé Mark Antony, and the woman that intoxicated them both. It was a worthy goal but one that the film, beset on all sides as it was, could no more than partially realize.

Part of the difficulty stems from the reality that *Cleopatra* is not one long narrative interrupted by an intermission but rather two quite different films. 20th Century-Fox, realizing this, gave serious consideration to releasing *Cleopatra* as two separate entities, but, bowing to the reality that the audience for the first part alone was close to non-existent, went the one big film route.

With the dignified, capable Rex Harrison cast as Caesar, it's inevitable that the first part of *Cleopatra*, detailing the measured realpolitik relationship between older Roman ruler and younger Egyptian queen, is more serious than what happens when the age-appropriate tabloid-fodder romance between her and Mark Antony takes center stage.

Here are some of Mankiewicz's better lines, zingers like "you stand here dribbling virtue out of the corner of your mouth" and Caesar's noting of Egypt's chief eunuch that his is "an exalted rank not obtained without certain sacrifices." But even during this part the stab at seriousness is both self-conscious and undercut by more boisterous scenes like Cleopatra arriving in Caesar's presence rolled in a rug, or her Greatest Show on Earth arrival in Rome on an enormous Sphinx-headed chariot pulled by hundreds of men. When Mark Antony says, "nothing like this has come into Rome since Romulus and Remus," he is not being hyperbolic.

Once Caesar is gone, conveniently assassinated by a group of Roman Senators led by, of all people, *All in the Family*'s Carrol O'Connor as Casca, the way is clear for Burton and Taylor, his football captain to her homecoming queen, to take center stage and give the audience, both then and now, what they've come to the movies for.

Whatever else is said about *Cleopatra*, the first kiss between these two remains a classic and the couple's scenes together are alive in the way the rest of this at times stodgy production (not to mention, with the notable exception of *Who's Afraid of Virginia Woolf*, their ten other theatrical features) manage to be.

Though not the bigger star, Burton is the more commanding performer. He holds the screen without effort, energizes Mark Antony with his great open smile and cocky charm, and masters lines like "everything I shall ever want to hold or look upon or have is here now with you." Of the aspects of *Cleopatra* that merit reconsideration, Burton's performance tops the list.

Taylor did not have her costar's acting credentials, but she was not the icon of her generation for nothing. Detractors could and did mock—Stanley Kauffman remarked that "she needs do no more than walk across the throne room to turn Alexandria into Beverly Hills"—but her energy and passion are unmistakable.

This is especially true in the scene where Cleopatra discovers that Mark Antony has married the pale Octavia (Jean Marsh, millennia away from her *Upstairs, Downstairs* career) and takes her revenge on their abandoned bed. According to David Kamp's encyclopedic article in *Vanity Fair*, Taylor shot the scene on the day Burton announced (prematurely as it turned out) that he would not leave his wife. In a tantrum that electrifies even today, "Taylor went at it with such gusto that she banged her hand and needed to go to the hospital for X rays. She was unable to work the next day."

Though it remains easy to laugh at this flawed film's expense, *Cleopatra* was hardly the fiasco its place in public memory would indicate. It was nominated for nine Oscars, including best actor for Harrison, and won in four categories (cinematography, art direction, costume design, and special effects).

And while everyone remembers the reviews that savagely attacked *Cleopatra* (Brendan Gill waspishly commented that the film "would have made a marvelous silent picture" and Judith Crist memorably skewered it as "at best a major disappointment, at worst an extravagant exercise in tedium"), the film got its share of positive notices, including a rave from *The New York Times*' powerful Bosley Crowther, who called it "one of the great epic films of our day."

Even in the all-important area of box office, *Cleopatra* eventually turned a profit despite its great cost, which is more than many of today's epics can say. With the public completely consumed by the Burton–Taylor liaison, *Cleopatra* became one of the highest grossing films of 1963, ended up playing in New York for sixty-three weeks, and went into profit in 1966 after ABC paid $5 million for television rights.

On one level the limited success *Cleopatra* achieved in the face of ungodly obstacles can be seen as a triumph of the system, the victory of industry worker bees over snarky gossipistas. But from another point of view the lesson of this film fifty years down the road is how little remembered that triumph is and the recognition of how often perception becomes reality in this town. It is the oldest of Hollywood lessons, and one we have to learn over and over again.

—Kenneth Turan

KENNETH TURAN is a film critic for the *Los Angeles Times* and National Public Radio's *Morning Edition*, as well as the director of the *Los Angeles Times* Book Prizes. A graduate of Swarthmore College, he teaches film reviewing and nonfiction writing at USC. His most recent books are *Free for All: Joe Papp, The Public, and the Greatest Theater Story Ever Told* and *Never Coming to a Theater Near You*.

Printed in the United States
by Baker & Taylor Publisher Services